そこでしかできない建築を考える｜プロジェクツ
Thinking of an Architecture for Nowhere but Here: Projects

目次	**Contents**

004	蓼科斜楼	004	Tateshina SHARO
008	川上村林業総合センター　森の交流館	008	Kawakami Forest Club
014	北総花の丘公園　花と緑の文化館	014	Hokuso Flower Park Center
018	逗子K邸	018	Zushi K House
022	名古屋大学	022	Nagoya University
	野依記念学術交流館		Noyori Conference Hall
	野依記念物質科学研究館		Noyori Materials Science Laboratory
	理学南館		Science South Building
	理農館		Science and Agricultural Building
034	ピア赤レンガ	034	Pier AKA-RENGA
038	龍谷大学	038	Ryukoku University
	深草キャンパス修景計画		Fukakusa Campus Landscape Project
	新1号館		Building 1
046	京急高架下文化芸術施設　日ノ出スタジオ	046	Hinode Studio
056	横須賀市営鴨居ハイム	056	Yokosuka Kamoi Public Housing
066	半居	066	HANKYO
076	パークハウス吉祥寺OIKOS	076	Park House Kichijoji OIKOS
080	新潟高田の家	080	House in Takada
084	沖縄県看護研修センター	084	Okinawa Nursing Training Center
092	京都府立新総合資料館（仮称）	092	Kyoto Prefectural Library and Archives [tentative name]

蓼科斜楼
Tateshina SHARO

1994

蓼科斜楼

蓼科の山中に建てられた別荘である。建物は大小2つのブロックからなる。

大きな方のブロックを占めるのは広間。南面のみが開放された筒状の空間で、天井が高くゆったりとした気積をもつ。床は敷地の傾斜に合わせて段状にレベルが変化していく。一方、小さなほうのブロックには寝室と浴室を収める。1階の寝室は窓の大きさを抑えた落ち着いた部屋なのに対し、2階の浴室は天井までガラスにした開放的な空間だ。

これらの諸室をつないでいるのが長いスロープで、南側の前庭から登って中へと侵入し、北端の土間前で折り返し、さらに登って南側のテラスへと至る。寝室と浴室は、このスロープの最下端と最上端に位置し、上下に重なっているにもかかわらず、その移動には建物内を端から端まで往復することになる。

スロープを支える構造は、張弦式鉄骨造の採用により最小化。スロープはそれ自体の存在感を打ち消しながらも、移動するという行為自体を視覚化している。森の中で木々の間をすり抜けて歩く体験を、そのまま空間構成へと翻案したかのような建築だ。

Tateshina SHARO

This is a second house located in a forest in Tateshina. The building comprises a large and small block. The bigger block is occupied by a spacious living room which is a tube space open only to the south with a high ceiling. The floor is stepped, varying to meet the sloping site. In the other volume, a bedroom and a bathroom are located. The bedroom on the first floor has a modest sized window with a calm ambience, however the bathroom on the second floor has a more open atmosphere with a window up to the ceiling.

A long ramp connects these spaces, which reach inside from a front yard to the south, and fold back in front of a doma (an exterior surface in the entrance area) at the north end, before climbing up to the terrace at the south. The bedroom and the bathroom are located at each end of this ramp, the lowest and the highest, so that even though they are on top of each other, one has to walk from one end of the building to the other.

The structure for this ramp is optimized using chord tensioned trusses, and this lightness allows it to almost disappear, but still express the action of movement. This is an architecture which translates the experience of walking through the forest into a spatial composition.

エントランスの土間を透かして屋内を見る
View of the interior through the entrance with doma

テラスから張り出した室内からつながる段上テラス
Exterior stairs extending from the terrace

広間の中を折り返して貫くスロープ
The slope zigzags through the spacious living room

Tateshina SHARO 1994

屋外の景色を楽しめる開かれた浴室
A light filled bathroom with views to the outdoors

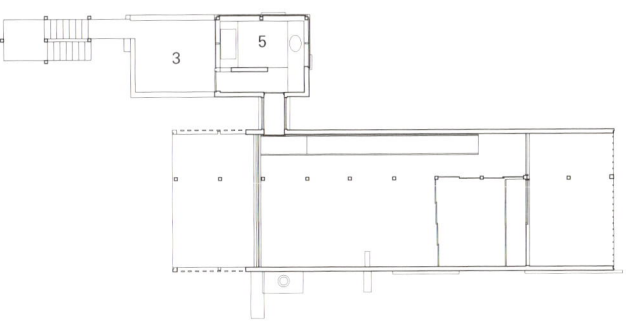

2階平面図　2F Plan

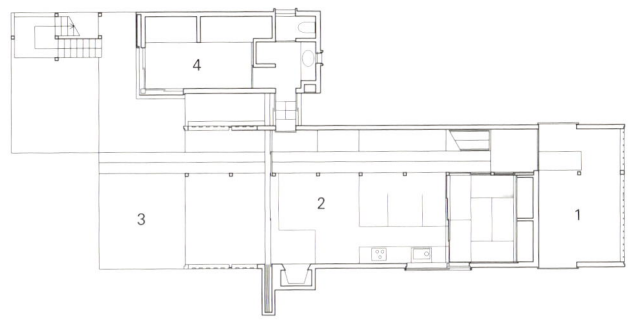

1階平面図　1F Plan　1:300

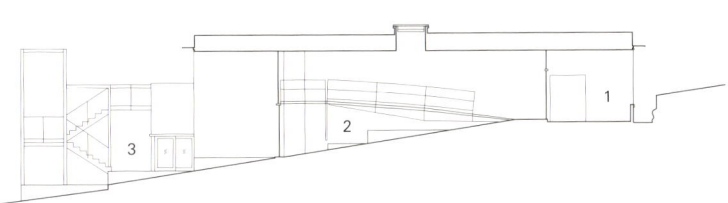

断面図　Section　1:300

1. エントランス（土間）
2. 広間
3. テラス
4. 寝室
5. 浴室

1. Entrance (Concrete Slab)
2. Living Room
3. Terrace
4. Bedroom
5. Bathroom

用途:別荘
設計期間:1993/10-1994/03
施工期間:1994/04-10
場所:長野県茅野市
延床面積:113.46㎡
構造:木造
階数:2/0

Use: Second House
Design Period: 10/1993-03/1994
Construction Period: 04-10/1994
Location: Chino City, Nagano
Total Floor Area: 113.46㎡
Structure: Wood
Floors: 2/0

川上村林業総合センター　森の交流館
Kawakami Forest Club

1997

カラマツ材の柱が林立するA棟の林業動植物研究学習室
Forestry, flora and fauna study room in annex A where larch columns stand like trees in the forest

川上村林業総合センター　森の交流館

Kawakami Forest Club

飯田善彦が初めて手がけた公共建築。高原野菜の産地として知られる長野県の川上村は、かつて林業で栄えていた。高度経済成長期の終わりとともに需要は減少し、外国産材の流入も相まって、林業は廃れた。しかし村にとって森林は、きれいな水をつくり、土砂崩れを防いでくれるかけがえのない存在である。これを守り育てて、新たに森の魅力を発信するべく、川上村林業総合センター「森の交流館」は計画された。

施設はA棟、B棟の2つからなる。A棟は川上村の林業について展示した棟で、2階にはレストランを併設している。B棟は森林組合の事務所や集会室などを収める。エントランスホールを介してつながる両棟は、前者が正方形平面でガラス張りの開放的な空間なのに対し、後者は東西に長い平面形で、外観もこの地方にある、せいろ倉を模した閉鎖的な建物と、対比的な構成となっている。

構造は木造に鉄骨や鉄筋コンクリートスラブなどを組み合わせたハイブリッド構造。特にB棟では、主構造に地場産のカラマツ材を使用している。それ以外にも内装、外装など、随所にカラマツ材が使われた。カラマツは反りや曲がりが起こりやすく、年月を経るとヤニも出るため、建築の材料としてあまり使われてこなかった。しかしこの建物では、設計の工夫により多様な場所にこれを使用。地元が育んだ森林の豊かさを、象徴的に表している。

飯田はこの作品で日本建築学会賞を受賞した。

This is Iida's first public building. Kawakami in Nagano is now known for highland vegetables, but once flourished with a forest timber industry. The demand for forest products declined at the end of the Post-War economic expansion period and also with the introduction of foreign timbers. However the forest is an invaluable asset for the village to produce beautiful pure water and to prevent landslide. This Kawakami forest club was planned to protect and promote the attractions of the forest once again.

The building consists of two annexes, A and B. A annex is mainly an exhibition space for the forestry of Kawakami and there is a restaurant on the second floor. The office for the forestry cooperative and their meeting room are in the B annex. The two annexes are connected with an entrance hall and have a contrasting composition. The former has a sense of openness, is square and covered with glass while the latter is a long rectangular enclosed building, running east west, and emulating a historical storage typology which is peculiar to this region.

A hybrid structure of timber, steel and RC slab is adopted. Especially in annex B, local larch is used for the main structure and also throughout for the interior and exterior finishes. Basically larch has not been popular as an architectural material because of its susceptibility to warping and twisting, and also because over time larch resin can leach out. However larch is used throughout this building by overcoming such problems with architectural ingenuity. It expresses the richness of the forest which the locals nurture. Mr. Iida was awarded the Architectural Institute of Japan prize for this project.

ボードウォークから見たA棟(左)とB棟。異なる素材やかたちが与えられている
View of annex A (left) and annex B from the board-walk, showing the different materials and forms

庭園から見たガラス張りのA棟
View from the garden, of the glass wall of annex A

下見板張りのB棟外壁
Exterior wall with clapboard siding on annex B

| 川上村林業総合センター　森の交流館 | Kawakami Forest Club | 1997 | 011 |

A棟2階のレストランから学習室の吹き抜けを見る
View of the double height space of the study room, looking from the restaurant on the second floor of annex A

B棟2階の林業技術員休憩室
The lounge for forestry technicians on the second floor of annex B

川上村林業総合センター　森の交流館　　Kawakami Forest Club　　1997　　013

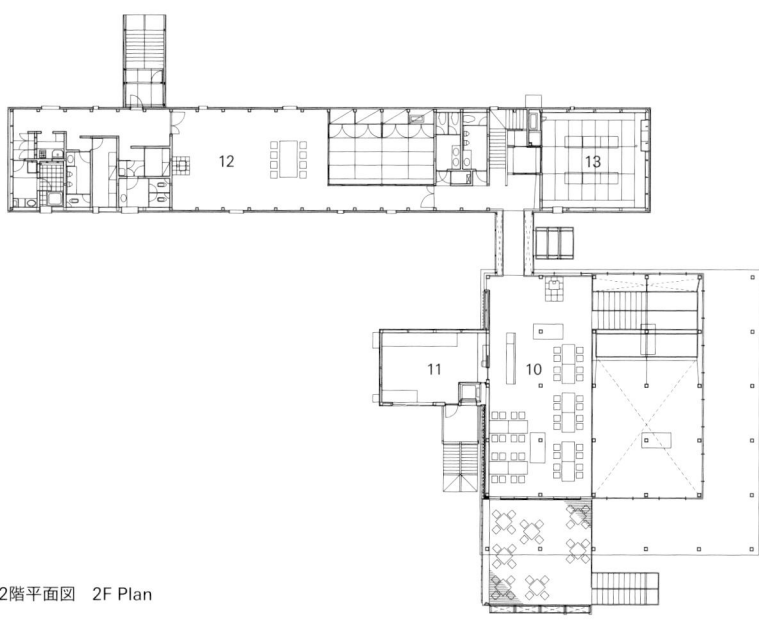

2階平面図　2F Plan

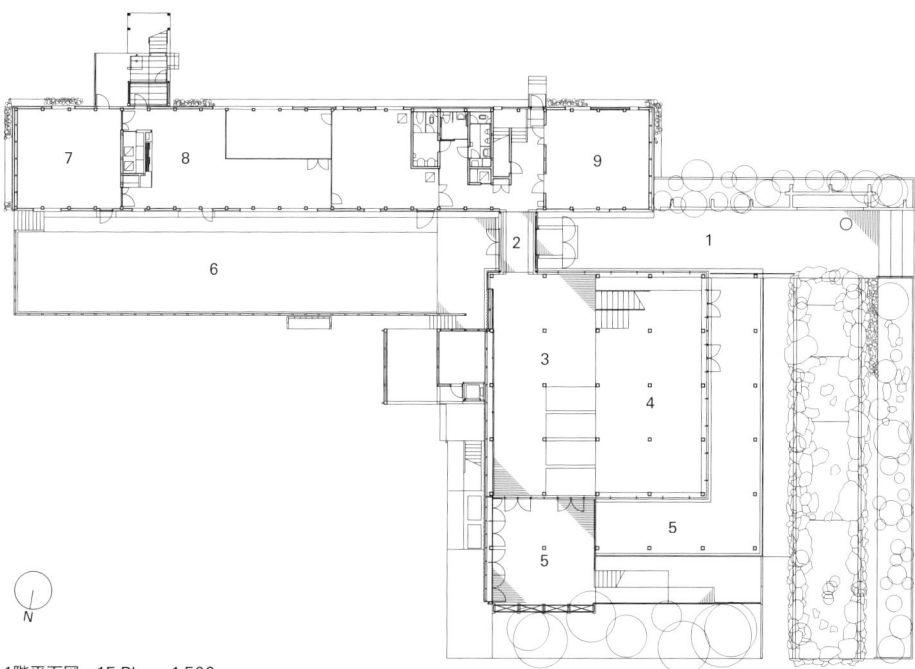

1階平面図　1F Plan　1:500

1. からまつボードウォーク
2. エントランス
3. 林業展示室
4. 林業動植物研究学習室
5. テラス
6. 造園展示コーナー
7. 機械保管庫・点検修理室
8. 林業組合オフィス
9. 研修室
10. レストラン
11. 厨房
12. 林業技術員休憩室
13. 会議室(和室)

1. Board-walk
2. Entrance
3. Forestry Exhibition Hall
4. Forestry, Flora and Fauna Study Room
5. Terrace
6. Gardening Exhibition Space
7. Machine Room
8. Office
9. Seminar Room
10. Restaurant
11. Kitchen
12. Forestry Technicians Lounge
13. Meeting Room (Japanese Room)

用途:地域交流施設
設計期間:1995/09-1996/07
施工期間:1996/09-1997/05
場所:長野県南佐久郡
延床面積:989.32㎡
構造:木造+鉄骨造
階数:2/0

Use: Community Center
Design Period: 09/1995-07/1996
Construction Period: 09/1996-05/1997
Location: Minamisaku-gun, Nagano
Total Floor Area: 989.32㎡
Structure: Wood+Steel Frame
Floors: 2/0

北総花の丘公園　花と緑の文化館
Hokuso Flower Park Center

2000

南西側から見た全景
View from the south west

北総花の丘公園　花と緑の文化館

千葉ニュータウンの一角、県立北総花の丘公園の中に建設された複合文化施設である。
この地域では、もともと花卉を栽培する農業が行われていた。そうした伝統的な産業と新しい住民とをつなぐ役割を果たすべく、施設では周辺に植生する植物の展示を行うほか、この地域に暮らす人への園芸活動に関するサポートを行う。運営にはボランティアが多くかかわり、地域コミュニティを活性化する機能も担っている。
建物は講習棟、情報棟、管理棟、展望棟など、機能ごとに独立している。それらを結びつけているのが、中央部のアーバンフラワープラザだ。大屋根の下のアトリウム空間は、展示温室であり、時にはイベントも開催される。異なる機能を結びつけることにより、新たなアクティビティを創発することが期待されている。その中を緩やかにカーブする道が通り抜け、外部へと連続する。そこに広がっているのは、三日月型のマウンドや重なりあう円弧状の園路による外構デザイン。建築とランドスケープの二重性をもった作品だ。

Hokuso Flower Park Center

This is a cultural facility located at Hokuso Flower Hill Garden in a corner of Chiba New Town.
This area has a history of flower cultivation and this facility takes the role of connecting the traditional horticultural industry and the new residents. It exhibits plants growing around the park and supports the horticultural activities of the local people. Many volunteers are involved in the operation, and so it is assuming the role of activation of the local community.
Annexes for lectures, information, management and viewing are independent by function, and the urban flower plaza in the center is connecting them. The atrium under a large roof is a greenhouse and occasionally events are held there. By connecting different functions, new activities are expected to be created here. A gently curving path is going through this atrium and continuing to the outside where a landscape design of a crescent formed mound and curving crossing paths spread out. This has the doubling characteristic of architecture and landscape.

展示温室とロビー、イベントホールを兼ねる「アーバンフラワープラザ」
'Urban Flower Plaza' functions as a Green House, Lobby and Event Hall

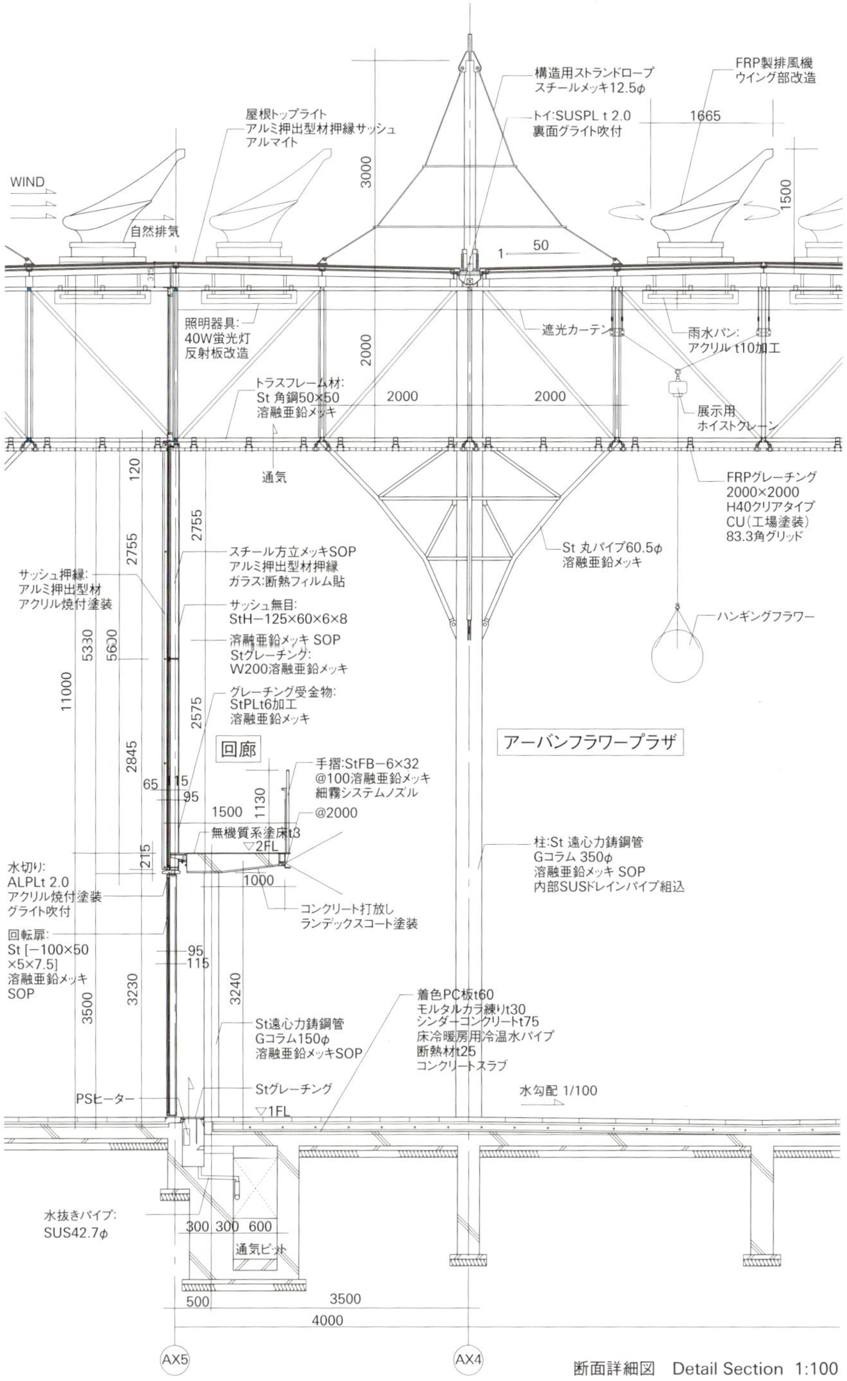

北総花の丘公園　花と緑の文化館　　Hokuso Flower Park Center　　2000　　017

池越しに見る情報棟
The information annex viewed from over the pond

複数の棟を結ぶペデストリアンデッキ
The pedestrian decking connecting several annexes

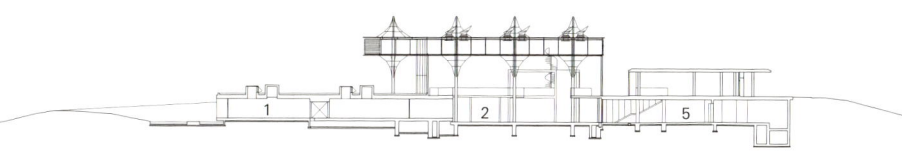
断面図　Section 1:1,000

1. 管理棟
2. アーバンフラワープラザ
3. 情報棟
4. 展望棟
5. 講習棟
6. 養生温室

1. Management Annex
2. Urban Flower Plaza
3. Information Annex
4. Viewing Annex
5. Lecture Annex
6. Nursery Greenhouse

用途：地域交流施設
設計期間：1997/11-1998/11
施工期間：1998/12-2000/03
場所：千葉県印西市
延床面積：2,762.20㎡
構造：鉄骨造＋SRC造＋RC造
階数：2/0

Use: Community Center
Design Period: 11/1997-11/1998
Construction Period: 12/1998-03/2000
Location: Inzai City, Chiba
Total Floor Area: 2,762.20㎡
Structure: Steel Frame+Steel Framed Reinforced Concrete+Reinforced Concrete
Floors: 2/0

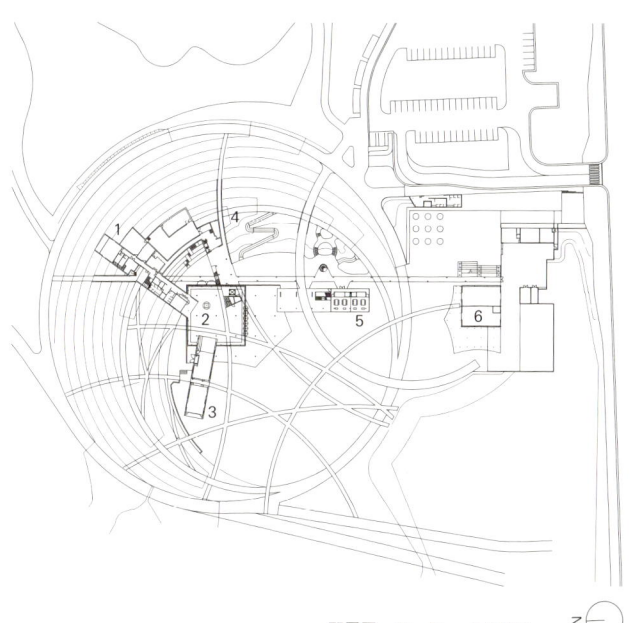
配置図　Site Plan 1:3,000

断面詳細図　Detail Section 1:100

逗子K邸
Zushi K House

2000

和室からコートテラスを介してリビングの方を見る。奥へと景色が重なっていく
Layered view from the Japanese room across the courtyard terrace toward the living room

逗子K邸

西側に富士山を望む台地状の住宅地に建てられた住宅。周囲には緑が多く残り、公園のようなエリアの中に位置している。

平面は3.6×5.4mのグリッドで、東西に2スパン、南北に3スパン。これが木造ラーメンの架構で2層に重なっている。西側は外に向けて全面が開放され、2階にはバルコニーが延びる。良好な外部環境を大きく取りこもうとする設計だ。

外観は1つの直方体として認識されるが、内部を注意深く眺めると、コートテラスを挟んで北側と南側の2つの領域に分かれている。1階では北側にリビング・ダイニング・キッチン、南側に和室を配し、両者がスロープで結ばれている。2階では北側の主寝室と南側の子供室が読書コーナーを挟んで振り分けられている。つまり蓼科斜楼や川上村林業総合センターと同じく、2つのブロックから成り立つ建築であるとも解釈できる。

Zushi K House

This is a house located on a terraced site in a residential area with views to Mt. Fuji in the west. The existing greenery is left intact and the surroundings are like a garden.

The plan is a 3.6 × 5.4m grid, with two spans in the east west direction, and three in the north south direction. A rigid-joint timber frame system is adopted and arranged in two layers. The west is all open to the outside and the balcony on the second floor stretches along this facade to bring the pleasant external environment inside.

The exterior is recognized as one cuboid, however looking at the inside carefully, there are two zones at the north and south with a court yard in between. On the first floor, a living, dining and kitchen area are at the north and a Japanese room at the south, and they are connected with a ramp. On the second floor, a main bedroom at the north and a children's room at the south are divided with a reading room. In fact we can construe this architecture as one which consists of two blocks just like Tateshina Shoroh and the Kawakami Forest Club.

前面道路から見た正面外観
View from the road

ブリッジ状に連続する2階バルコニーから主寝室を見る
View of the main bedroom from the balcony on the second floor, which continues like a bridge

2階の読書スペース。浴室を通して豊かな緑が見える
The reading space on the second floor. Abundant greenery can be seen from the bathroom

021

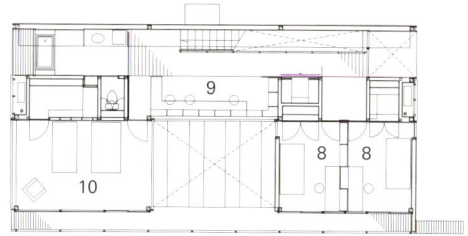

2階平面図　2F Plan

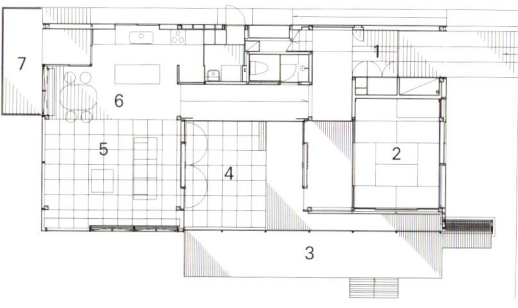

1. エントランス
2. 和室
3. バルコニー
4. コートテラス
5. リビング
6. ダイニング
7. キッチンテラス
8. 子供室
9. 読書スペース
10. 寝室

1. Entrance
2. Japanese Room
3. Balcony
4. Court Terrace
5. Living Room
6. Dining Room
7. Kitchen Terrace
8. Kid's Room
9. Reading Space
10. Bedroom

1階平面図　1F Plan　1:300

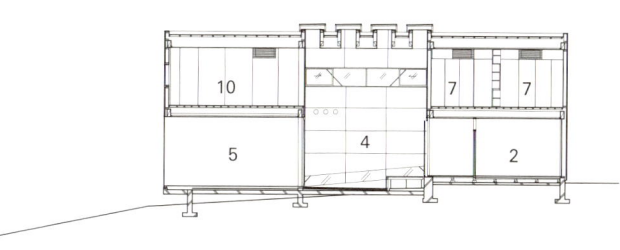

断面図　Section　1:300

用途:住宅
設計期間:1999/05-10
施工期間:1999/12-2000/07
場所:神奈川県逗子市
延床面積:219.42㎡
構造:木造
階数:2/0

Use: Residence
Design Period: 05-10/1999
Construction Period: 12/1999-07/2000
Location: Zushi City, Kanagawa
Total Floor Area: 219.42㎡
Structure: Wood
Floors: 2/0

名古屋大学
Nagoya University

2003, 2011

野依記念学術交流館の3階ゲストハウス外観
The guest house on the third floor of the Noyori Conference Hall

名古屋大学

野依記念学術交流館
野依記念物質科学研究館
理学南館
理農館

野依記念学術交流館と野依記念物質科学研究館は、名古屋大学理学部教授の野依良治氏がノーベル化学賞を受賞したことを記念して同時に企画された。設計者選定は日本建築学会作品賞の受賞者を参加資格としたプロポーザルによって行われ、応募した18人の中から飯田善彦が選ばれた。

2棟は、かたちも機能も異なる。物質科学研究館は研究室や実験室のほかレクチャーホールと展示室を収めた建物。一方、広場を挟んで建つ学術交流館は、人工地盤のような床を挟んで下にレクチャーホールと情報ラウンジ、上に海外から招聘した研究者が滞在するゲストハウスを収める。異なる機能とかたちをもつ2つのブロックがつかず離れずの関係で隣り合う関係は、物質科学研究館と学術交流館の2棟とも共通。さらには公道を挟んで東西2つのエリアに分かれる大学キャンパスとも相似形の関係をもつ。「対の関係」が入れ子状に連関しながら、建築から周辺環境へと広がっていくという構造だ。

続いて名古屋大学の理学部出身者3人が、相次いでノーベル賞を受賞。それが後押しとなって、野依記念物質科学研究館に隣接して理学南館と理農館が建設された。こちらも内部には研究室やレクチャーホールを容れている。ファサードにはステンレスメッシュやFRPグレーチングを使用、野依記念物質科学研究館の建物から連続させることで、まとまりを生み出している。

Nogoya University

Noyori Conference Hall
Noyori Materials Science Laboratory
Science South Building
Science and Agricultural Building

The Noyori Conference Hall and Noyori Materials Science Laboratory have been established to commemorate Nagoya University School of Science professor Ryoji Noyori, the Nobel laureate in chemistry. The design competition for these buildings was open to those architects who had won the Architectural Institute of Japan prize. 18 architects competed and Mr. Iida was selected. The two buildings are different in their function and form. The Materials Science Laboratory contains laboratories, experimental laboratories, lecture halls and exhibition rooms. On the other hand, the Conference Hall across the square has a lecture hall and information lounge under an artificial groundlike floor with a guest house for invited foreign researchers above. The relationship of these two volumes, with differences in function and form, and which are neighboring but maintain a cautious distance, is the same as that of the Conference Hall and Materials Science Laboratory. Furthermore it has a similarity to the relationship between the two campuses which are located to the east and west with a public road in between. This paired relationship is embedded and related, and spreads from the architecture to the surrounding environment.

Subsequently three graduates from Nagoya university school of science have won the Nobel Prize one after another, and this result has encouraged construction of the Science South Building and Science and Agricultural Building. Laboratories and lecture halls are also accommodated here. Stainless mesh and FRP grating are used for the facade and this generates a cohesion by continuing the vocabulary of the Noyori Materials Science Laboratory.

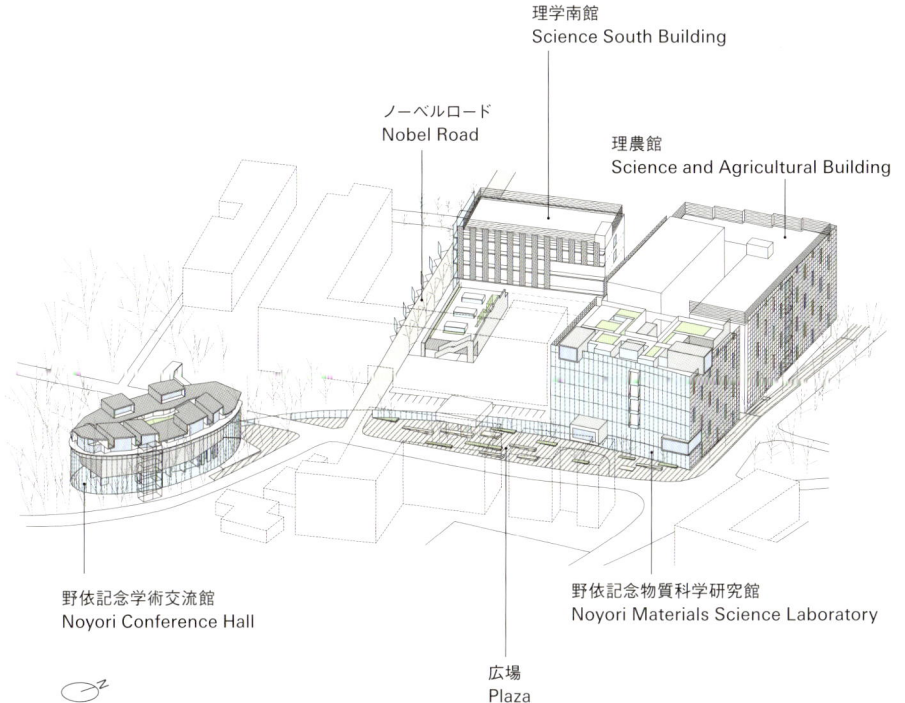

理学南館
Science South Building

ノーベルロード
Nobel Road

理農館
Science and Agricultural Building

野依記念学術交流館
Noyori Conference Hall

野依記念物質科学研究館
Noyori Materials Science Laboratory

広場
Plaza

野依記念学術交流館
Noyori Conference Hall

2003

カフェを併設したエントランスロビー
Entrance lobby with café

雑木林に内包される1階、南側のラウンジ
The lounge to the south on the first floor surrounded by forest

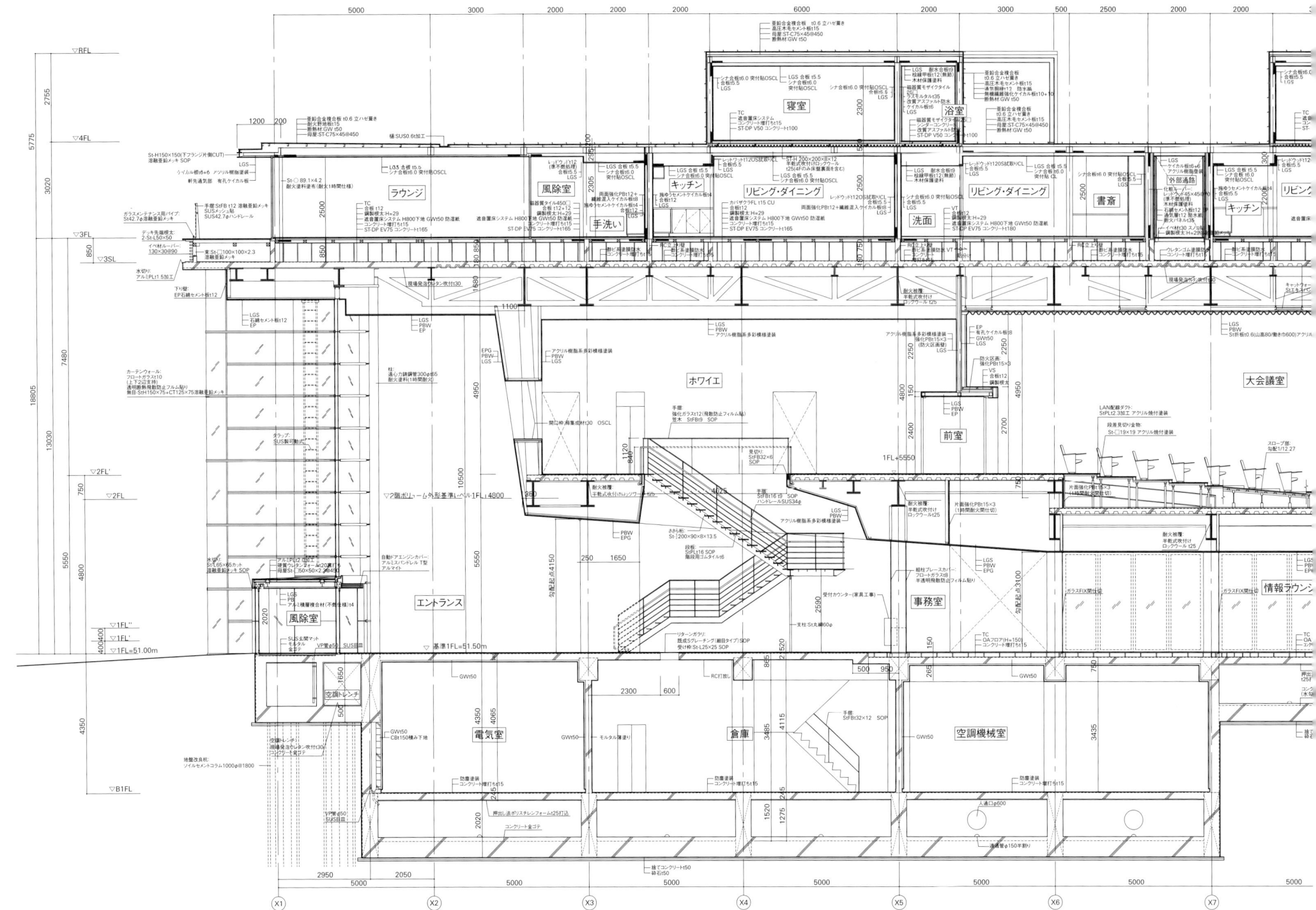

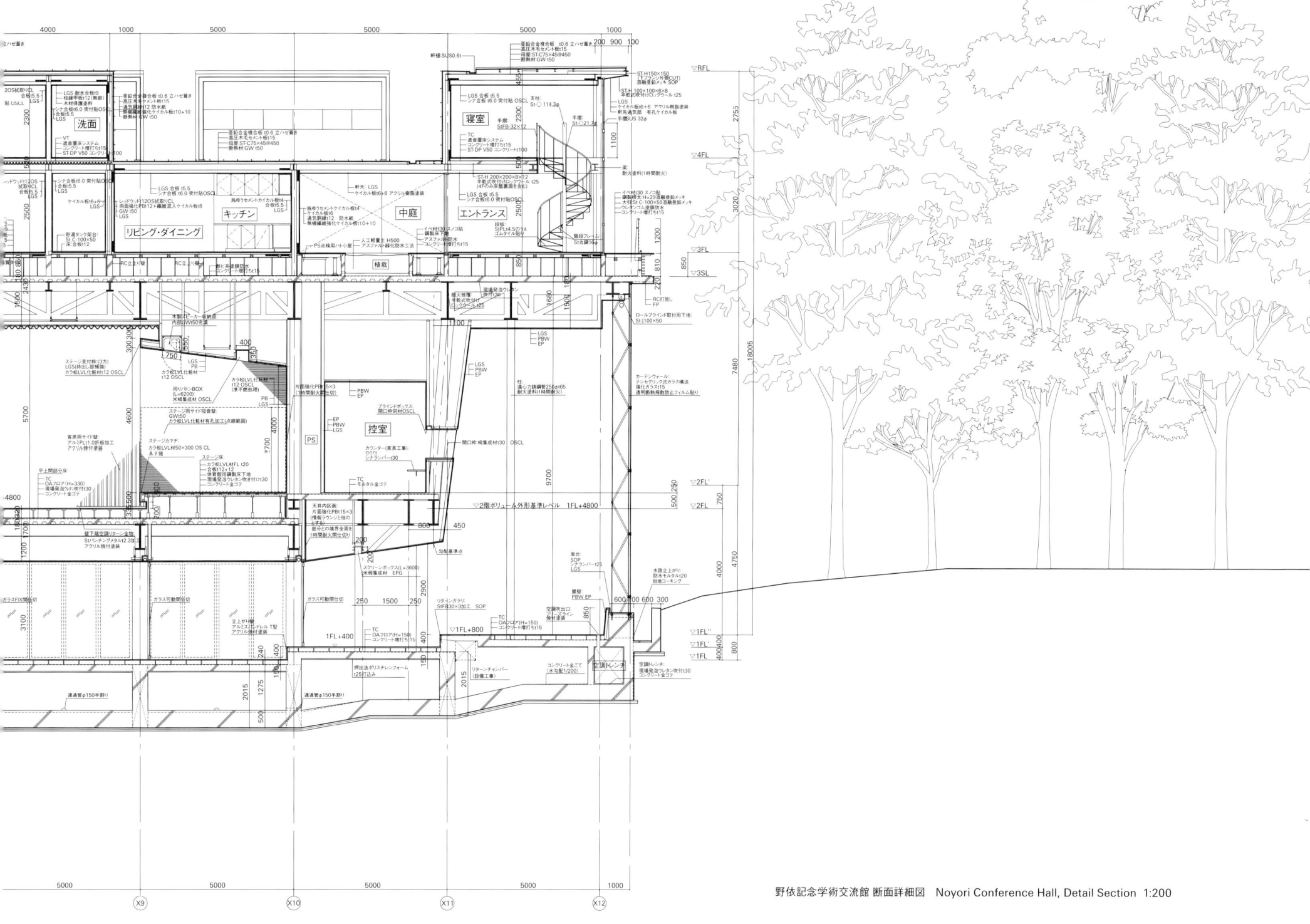

野依記念学術交流館 断面詳細図　Noyori Conference Hall, Detail Section 1:200

北東側から見た夕景
Evening view from the north east

野依記念学術交流館　Noyori Conference Hall　2003

3階、ゲストハウスに囲まれた中庭
The courtyard surrounded by guest houses on the third floor

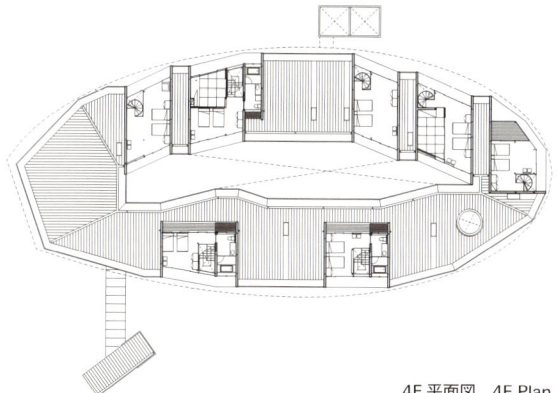

4F 平面図　4F Plan

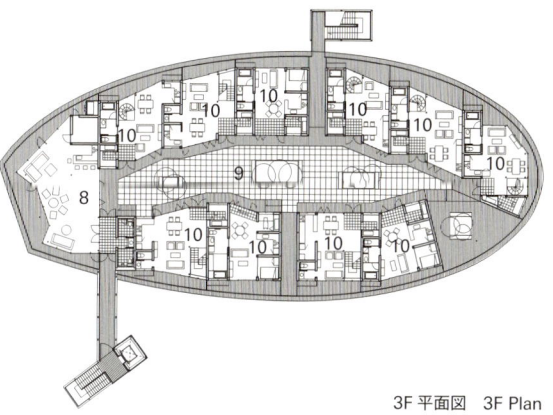

3F 平面図　3F Plan

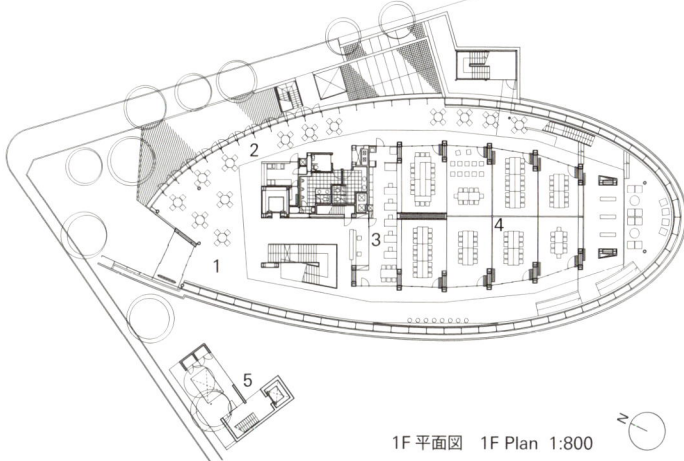

1F 平面図　1F Plan　1:800

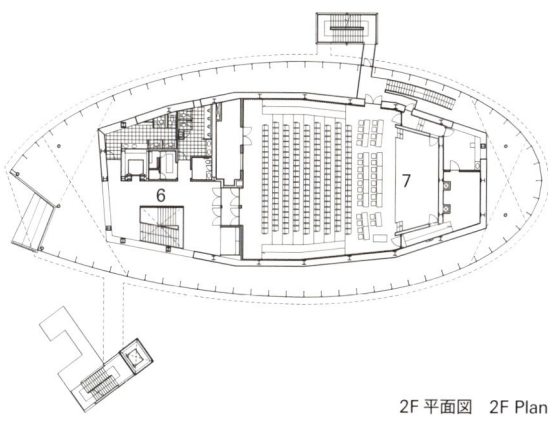

2F 平面図　2F Plan

1. エントランスロビー　1. Entrance Lobby
2. カフェ　2. Café
3. 事務室　3. Office
4. 情報ラウンジ　4. Information Lounge
5. 住居棟エントランス　5. Guest House Level Entrance
6. ホワイエ　6. Foyer
7. ホール　7. Hall
8. ラウンジ　8. Lounge
9. 中庭　9. Courtyard
10. ゲストハウス　10. Guest House

野依記念物質科学研究館
Noyori Materials Science Laboratory

2003

セラミックプリントのガラスで覆われた南東側ファサード
The south east facade covered with ceramic printed glass

ステンレスメッシュで覆われた北東側ファサード
The north east facade covered with stainless mesh

FRPグレーチングで覆われた南西側ファサード
The south west facade covered with FRP grating

理学南館
Science South Building

2011

キャンパス内のメイン・ストリート「ノーベルロード」に面したファサード。歩行者から講堂内部が見える
The facade facing the 'Nobel Road' which is the main street in the campus. Pedestrians can see the inside of the lecture hall

ブナ積層材のリブで覆われた講堂内観
The interior of the lecture hall covered with fine laminated beech ribs

理農館
Science and Agricultural Building

2011

低層部に横ルーバー、高層部に縦ルーバーが
取り付けられた南西側のファサード
The south west facade with lower louvers
running horizontally and the upper louvers
running vertically

野依記念学術交流館
用途:ホール+レジデンス
設計期間:2002/04-10
施工期間:2002/11-2003/11
場所:愛知県名古屋市
延床面積:3,485.00㎡
構造:鉄骨造
階数:4/1

野依記念物質科学研究館
用途:研究棟+記念館
設計期間:2002/04-10
施工期間:2002/11-2003/12
場所:愛知県名古屋市
延床面積:7,117.00㎡
構造:SRC造
階数:7/1

理農館・理学南館
用途:実験棟・研究棟
設計期間:2009/04-11
施工期間:
理農館=2010/01-2011/07
理学南館=2010/04-2011/03
場所:愛知県名古屋市
延床面積:
理農館=9,322.94㎡
理学南館=3,960.64㎡
構造:
理農館=SRC造
理学南館=RC造+鉄骨造
階数:
理農館=6/1+塔屋1/0
理学南館=5/1+塔屋5/0
共同設計:名古屋大学施設管理部

Noyori Conference Hall
Use: Hall+Residence
Design Period: 04-10/2002
Construction Period: 11/2002-11/2003
Location: Nagoya City, Aichi
Total Floor Area: 3,485.00㎡
Structure: Steel Frame
Floors: 4/1

Noyori Materials Science Laboratory
Use: Laboratory Block+Museum
Design Period: 04-10/2002
Construction Period: 11/2002-12/2003
Location: Nagoya City, Aichi
Total Floor Area: 7,117.00㎡
Structure: Steel Framed Reinforced Concrete
Floors: 7/1

Science and Agricultural Building [A]
Science South Building [B]
Use: Laboratory+Research Block
Design Period: 04-11/2009
Construction Period:
[A]=01/2010-07/2011
[B]=04/2010-03/2011
Location: Nagoya City, Aichi
Total Floor Area:
[A]=9,322.94㎡ ; [B]=3,960.64㎡
Structure:
[A]=Steel Framed Reinforced Concrete
[B]=Reinforced Concrete+Steel Frame
Floors:
[A]=6/1+Solar Chimney, 1/0
[B]=5/1+Solar Chimney, 5/0
Collaborator: Facilities Department of Nagoya University

ピア赤レンガ
Pier AKA-RENGA

2004

陸側から見た全景
View from landward

ピア赤レンガ

横浜の名所、赤レンガ倉庫の先に設けられたシーバスの桟橋施設。船の乗客のための小さな待合所が設置されている。観光の拠点でもあることからデザイン性に優れたものとすることが求められたが、一方では横浜港大さん橋国際客船ターミナルに間近いこともあり、目立ち過ぎないことも意図された。その結果、実現したのがこの鉄板でできた建物で、実は桟橋と一体化したものを造船所で製作し、それを曳航してきて現場で打設した杭に取り付けるという工法を採っている。丸窓や内装のフローリングなども、船のデザインを強く意識させるもの。限りなく船に近い建築だ。
横浜に事務所を構えて6年目だった飯田善彦は、この都市の重要なゾーンで、小さな建物ながらその設計者として参画することができたことに、喜びを感じたことを漏らしている。

Pier AKA-RENGA

This is a ticketing and waiting space on a pier for a sea-bus beside the famous red brick warehouse in Yokohama. A high-quality design was required since this is a hub for sightseeing, but at the same time it needed to be discrete as the Osanbashi Yokohama International Passenger Terminal is nearby. As a result this building made with steel plates is integrated with the pier, built at a shipyard and towed to the site and moored. The round windows and interior flooring is informed by nautical design. This is an architecture very much like a ship.
Six years had passed since Mr. Iida shifted his office to Yokohama, and he mentioned that he felt pleasure in designing even a small project in this very important part of the city.

赤レンガ倉庫やみなとみらい地区を背景に望む
View of Pier AKA-RENGA with brick warehouses and Minato Mirai District in the background

造船所での建造中の様子
Under construction at the shipyard

ピア赤レンガ　　　　　Pier AKA-RENGA　　　　　2004　　　　　037

用途：船舶発着待合所
設計期間：2003/12-2004/01
施工期間：2003/12-2004/03
場所：神奈川県横浜市
延床面積：54.44㎡
構造：鉄骨造
階数：1/0

Use: Sea-bus Terminal
Design Period: 12/2003-01/2004
Construction Period: 12/2003-03/2004
Location: Yokohama City, Kanagawa
Total Floor Area: 54.44㎡
Structure: Steel Frame
Floors: 1/0

床、壁、天井ともフローリングで仕上げられた内観
The interior view showing timber flooring on the floor, walls and ceiling

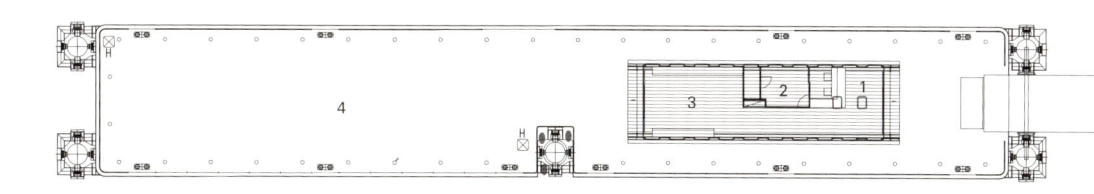

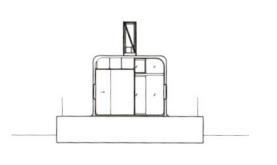

断面図　Section 1:400

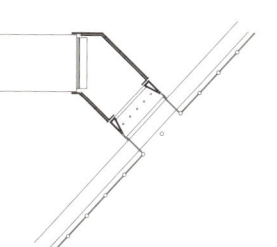

平面図　Plan 1:400

1. チケットカウンター
2. スタッフルーム
3. ロビー
4. ポンツーン

1. Ticket Counter
2. Staff Room
3. Lobby
4. Pontoon

Ryukoku University

2006 2015

修景計画が実施された中庭の全景
View of the landscaped courtyard

龍谷大学

深草キャンパス修景計画
新1号館

1960年に開設された龍谷大学深草キャンパスの再整備計画に、飯田善彦は一貫してかかわっている。最初にかかわったのは中庭の修景計画だった。情報キオスク、ステージ、水盤、回廊、テラスなどを配置し、アクティビティを可視化させると同時に、形態として円を多用することで、バラバラだった校舎群にまとまりを与えることにも成功している。

その後に実施されたキャンパス施設整備計画プロポーザルで、飯田は1等を獲得。最初に建設される新1号館では、それまでの壁に囲まれた「ボックスタイプ」の建物から、積層する床とコアで構成され「スラブタイプ」の建築へと変えることにより、内外に自由に活動を展開できるようにする。また、既存の校舎とつなぐしかけとして、縁側のようなコモンリングを中庭側に巡らせることを提案している。

そのほか、地域と結びつく拠点として新エクステンションセンター、新学友会館、新体育館などの施設をキャンパス周辺に計画。

これら全体のプロジェクトを進めるために、大学側の担当者と設計者、施工者が、設計から一体となった建築の仕組みを考案し、緊密な連携による柔軟な体制を取ることによりコストの削減も図っている。

Ryukoku University

Fukakusa Campus Landscape Project
Building 1

Mr. Iida has been consistently involved in the renewal projects of Ryukoku University Fukakusa Campus which opened in 1960. His first involvement was the landscaping of a central courtyard. He designed the information kiosk, stage, water pond, cloister and terrace to facilitate and view the various activities and at the same time he was successful in giving a cohesion to the groups of disjointed buildings by using many circles as a formative strategy. Mr. Iida won the competition for the campus renewal afterward. He introduced a slab-type architecture which consists of layers of floors and a core, not a box-type architecture surrounded with walls. This made it possible for students to develop their activities freely from the inside to the outside. He also proposed a series of rings which works just like an Engawa around the center courtyard to connect with the existing buildings.
In addition, as a base to connect with the community, a new extension center, a new student hall and a new gymnasium are planned to be built on the periphery of the campus.
To proceed with this entire project, the university, the architect and also the contractors have been discussing widely the architectural issues throughout and this has helped to reduce the project cost.

深草キャンパス修景計画
Fukakusa Campus Landscape Project

2006

円形のステージとそれにつながる回廊
The cloister connected to the circular stage

回廊から円形ステージを見る。GRCパネルの屋根材
View of the circular stage from the cloister. GRC panels are used on the roof

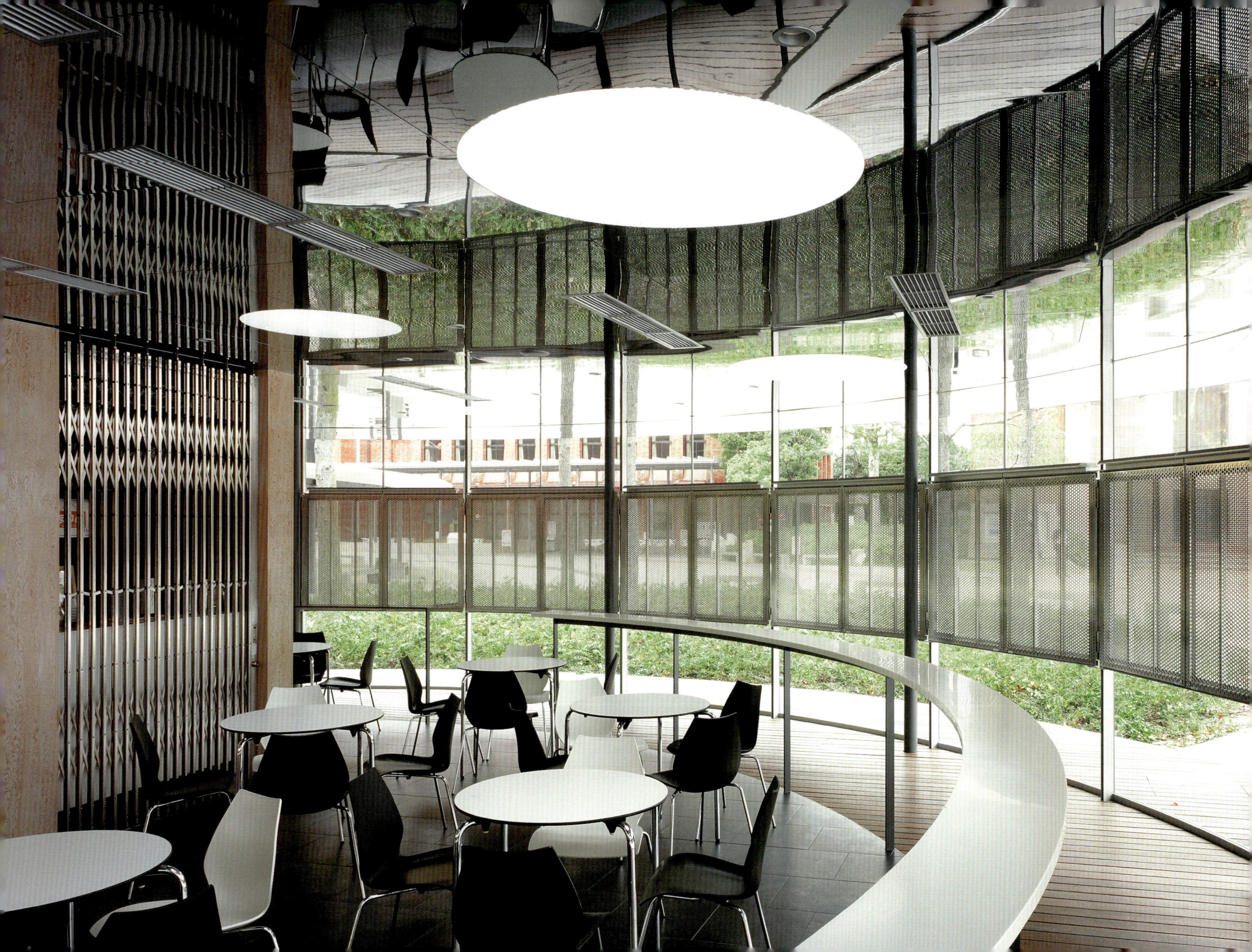

生協前テラス
The terrace in front of the co-op

天井に周囲が映り込む情報キオスクの内観
The interior of the kiosk with a ceiling that reflects the surroundings

新1号館
Building 1

2015

建設途中を東側から見る
View from the east during construction

045

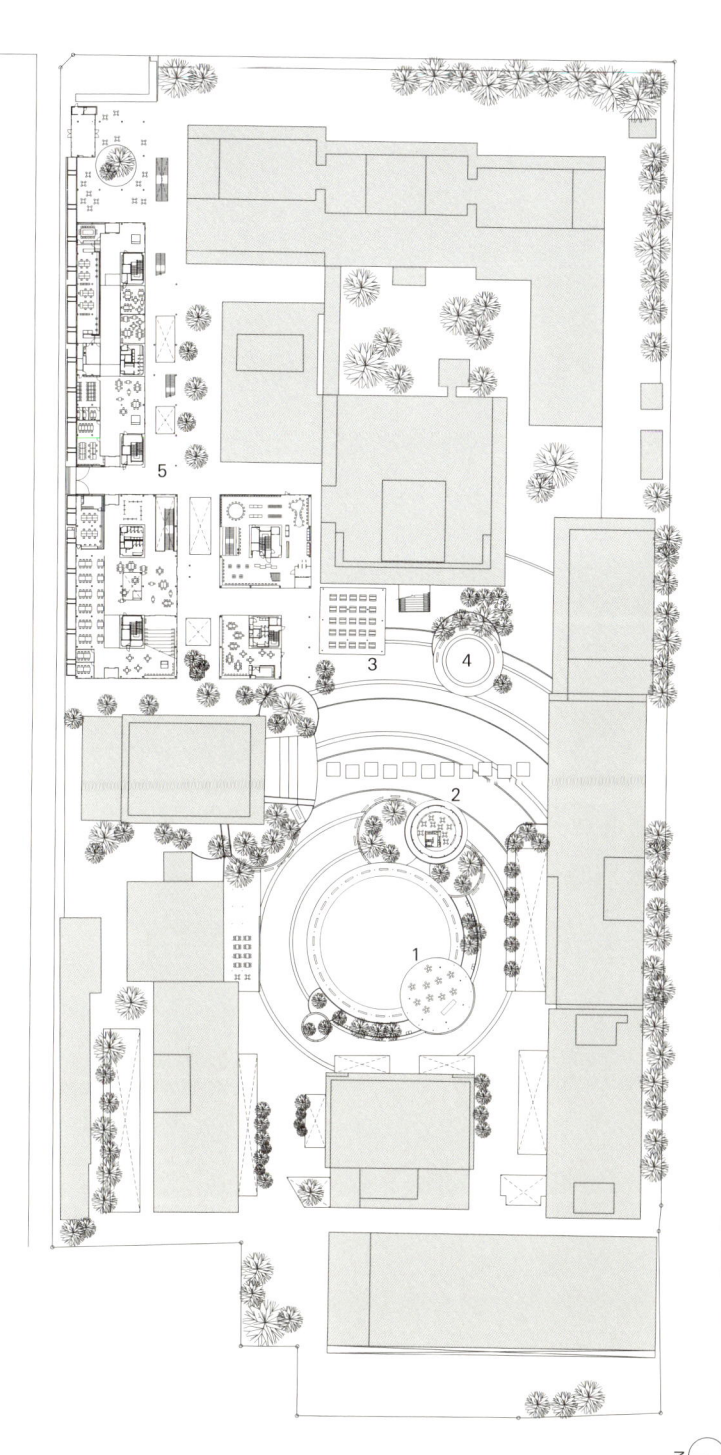

深草キャンパス施設整備計画の全体模型
The overall model of the Fukakusa Campus Landscape Project

1. ステージ
2. 情報キオスク（カフェ）
3. 図書館テラス
4. 池
5. 新1号館

1. Stage
2. Information Kiosk (Café)
3. Library Terrace
4. Pond
5. Building 1

深草キャンパス修景計画
用途：ランドスケープ
設計期間：2004/03-2005/06
施工期間：2005/08-2006/10
場所：京都府京都市
総工事面積：15,380.00㎡
延床面積：944.70㎡
構造：鉄骨造＋RC造
階数：1/0

新1号館
用途：図書館＋講義棟
設計期間：2012/04-2013/01
施工期間：2013/03-2015/01
場所：京都府京都市
延床面積：27,643.65㎡
構造：RC造＋鉄骨造＋SRC造
階数：6/2

Fukakusa Campus Landscape Project
Use: Landscape
Design Period: 03/2004-06/2005
Construction Period: 08/2005-10/2006
Location: Kyoto City, Kyoto
Total Construction Area: 15,380.00㎡
Total Floor Area: 944.70㎡
Structure: Steel Frame+Reinforced Concrete
Floors: 1/0

Building 1
Use: Library+Lecture Block
Design Period: 04/2012-01/2013
Construction Period: 03/2013-01/2015
Location: Kyoto City, Kyoto
Total Floor Area: 27,643.65㎡
Structure: Reinforced Concrete+Steel Frame+Steel Framed Reinforced Concrete
Floors: 6/2

配置図　Site Plan　1:2,000

京急高架下文化芸術施設　日の出スタジオ　　　　2008

Hinode Studio

大岡川側全景。スタジオ上部は京浜急行の高架。大岡川には船着場がある
View of Ooka river. The Keihin Kyuko railway running above the studios. There are boat slips along Ooka river

京急高架下文化芸術施設　日ノ出スタジオ

Hinode Studio

鉄道の高架下を有効利用した、アーティストの制作スタジオや展示場。敷地は大岡川に面してサクラ並木が続く美しい景観を備える一方、違法な風俗店舗も多く集まっており、都市の中心部にありながら足を踏み入れにくいエリアだった。京浜急行が高架の耐震改修工事を完了させたのを受け、その下の空間でアート関連の活動を行い、人を呼び込んで街を変えていくことが目指された。飯田は、教鞭をとっていた横浜国立大学大学院／建築都市スクール"Y-GSA"が横浜市のまちづくりに携わる協定を結んだのをきっかけに、これにかかわった。

敷地となる高架下には、5.4×3.6mの間隔で太い柱が並んでいる。この構造から、施設は完全に独立でなければならない。平面計画における大きな制約と法規制限をクリアするために、飯田が採ったのは、川上村林業総合センターや花と緑の文化館などと同じく、分棟の形式だった。

ここでは大きさや平面の異なる3棟を並べ、それを屋上通路で結んで、一体感をもたせている。建物の隙間や屋上通路は、イベントの際にも使われる。アーティストに、その使い方を触発させる空間だ。

この施設と同時に、近くの同じ高架下に黄金町スタジオ（設計：みかんぐみ）も完成した。その後も周囲には続々とアート関連施設が増え、イベント開催も定期的に。街は着実に、変わってきている。

A workshop and gallery for artists uses the space under the elevated central railway efficiently. The site has beautiful scenery with a row of cherry trees along Ooka river, however one needs a moments pause before entering this area in the center of the city because there are many illegal adult-entertainment shops here. When the Keikyu Line completed the seismic retrofitting, it aimed to change this town by attracting more people through art related activities under the elevated railway. Mr. Iida started to get involved in this project since Yokohama Graduate School of Architecture (Y-GSA) forged a pact with Yokohama City regarding town planning when he was teaching there. Heavy structural columns are lined up on a 5.4m × 3.6m grid under the railway. The new facility had to be completely independent of this structure. Mr. Iida chose to use the same vocabulary – annex system - as Kawakami Forest Club and Hokuso Flower Park Center, to comply with legal restrictions and planning limitations.

Three annexes with various floor shapes and sizes are lined up and connected with elevated passages to bring a sense of unity. The spaces in between the annexes and the elevated passages are used for events. This space sets off artists to think about how to use it.

The Kogane-cho Studio (designed by MIKAN) under the elevated railway nearby was also completed at the same time. The number of art related facilities has been increasing steadily in this area, and events have been held constantly. This city has been steadily changing.

スタジオは高架下に配置されている。高架は道路が並走し、道行く人が立ち寄る
The studios are located under the elevated railway. The road runs parallel to the railway and passengers stop by

高架裏の天井を間近に見上げながら歩く屋上の通路
The walk way on the roof looking up to the ceiling of the railway

イベントにも使われる棟間のスペース。上下に人が交錯する
The spaces between the studios which are used for events. Paths cross…

屋上通路からガラス越しに見下ろすショップ
A shop viewed from the walk way on the roof through the glass

ショップ内から見上げる屋上通路
The walk way on the roof looking up from a shop

ショップ内が見渡せる外観
The street view which shows pedestrians looking into the interior

外の景色が見渡せるショップ壁面
From the interior the outside scenery can been viewed

高架の太い柱の回りに取り付いている本棚什器
Book shelf around the columns supporting the railway above

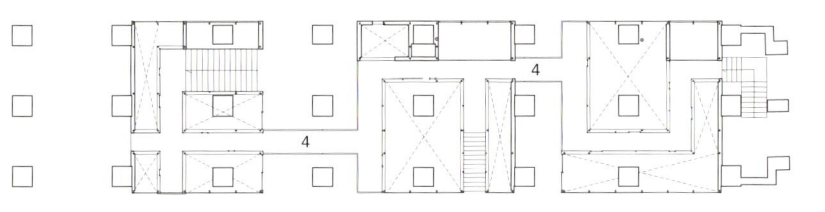

1F 平面図　1F Plan 1:400

2F 平面図　2F Plan 1:400

京急高架下文化芸術施設　日の出スタジオ　　Hinode Studio　　2008　　053

テナントとして入っているアトリエ
The atelier in the tenant space

屋上通路へと上がる北側の外部階段とショップ入口
Shop entrance and exterior stair at the north which leads to the walk way on the roof

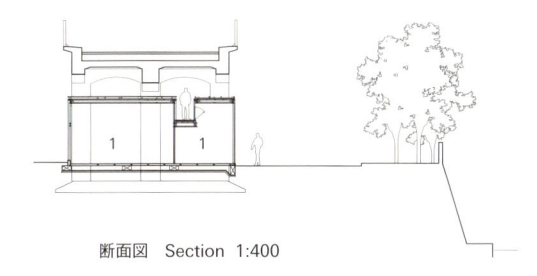

断面図　Section 1:400

1. スタジオ
2. イベントスペース
3. キッチン
4. 屋上通路

1. Studio
2. Event Space
3. Kitchen
4. Roof Top Walkway

用途：ギャラリー＋アートスタジオ
設計期間：2007/08-2008/04
施工期間：2008/05-08
場所：神奈川県横浜市
延床面積：212.07㎡
構造：鉄骨造
階数：1/0
共同設計：横浜国立大学大学院／建築都市スクール
"Y-GSA" 飯田善彦スタジオ＋SALHAUS

Use: Gallery+Art Studio
Design Period: 08/2007-04/2008
Construction Period: 05-08/2008
Location: Yokohama City, Kanagawa
Total Floor Area: 212.07㎡
Structure: Steel Frame
Floors: 1/0
Collaborator: Yoshihiko Iida Studio, Y-GSA; SALHAUS

大岡川越しに見る夕景
Night view over Ooka river

夜の大岡川を建物が行灯のように照らす
The buildings are lighting Ooka river like a lantern

横須賀市営鴨居ハイム 2009
Yokosuka Kamoi Public Housing

D

横須賀市営鴨居ハイム

1950年代に建設された市営住宅団地の建て替え。公募方式のエスキスコンペによって、飯田善彦が設計者として選ばれ、足掛け7年にわたるプロジェクトを完遂した。

新しい市営住宅団地では、2〜3階建ての住棟が適度な間隔で並んでいる。2DKの住戸を2戸ずつ組み合わせた建物を基本的な単位とし、1LDK、3DK、4DKなどの住戸バリエーションも用意した。60歳以上を対象とするシルバーハウジング棟も組み込まれている。高齢者のための生活相談室は、市営住宅の集会室と向かい合わせることにより、世代間の交流も促している。

敷地の中は、既存の水路や公道に並行して通路が東西に敷地を貫く一方、中庭はそれに直交して南北に並行している。オープンスペースが縦横に走って敷地全体を覆う様子は、織物のようだ。そこにベンチや植物などが添えられ、良好な外部環境を生み出している。

建て替え前は、平屋の住宅群が道や庭と分かち難く一体化し、風景をつくり上げていた。住戸数は80戸から160戸へと倍増するが、設計者は従来の住環境の良さを、建て替えで失うことなく継承しようと目論んだ。その意図は確かに実践されたと言えるだろう。

Yokosuka Kamoi Public Housing

This is a rebuild project of pablic-housing built in the 1950's. Mr. Iida was chosen as the architect by an open sketchdesign competition, and he completed this project over seven years.

In this newly built complex, two or three story apartments are lining up with adequate spaces between. Apartments are mirrored and typically two rooms + Dining and Kitchen (2DK) but there are also 1LDK, 3DK and 4DK configurations.

Housing for people over 60 years old is also included. A consulting room for the elderly is facing the meeting room for this whole complex to promote exchanges among the generations.

A path is running through the site parallel to an existing water channel and road are running through the site east west, but the courtyard is perpendicular to them, lying north south. The open spaces crisscross the site just like fabric. Benches and plants are prepared and it generates a quality and comfortable outside environment.

Before this was rebuilt, single story housing was united with the road and gardens, and that created its own scenery. The number of houses have been doubled from 80 to 160, Mr. Iida strove to improve the original good living environment. We believe that his intention has been achieved successfully.

3階建て(一部メゾネット4階建て)の住棟
A three story annex (plus maisonette)

敷地内を南北に貫く緑道
The green passage running north south through the site

敷地内を東西に流れる小川の両脇に敷かれたウッドデッキ
Wooden decking along both sides of the stream running east west through the site

低層住棟の間をぬう緑道に連続していく、居住者の生活環境
A living environment continues to the green passage which runs through the lower annexes

子どもが集まって遊ぶ集会所付近
Children are playing around the assembly room

横須賀市営鴨居ハイム　　Yokosuka Kamoi Public Housing　　2009

住棟に向けて全面開口される集会所の和室
A Japanese tatami room open to the surrounding residential buildings

みんなが利用する緑道のベンチ
Benches in the green passage everyone can use

生活感あふれる軒先の植木鉢
A stack of flower pots full of life under the eaves

出会いのあるバス停の大ベンチ
A long bench at a bus stop where people can meet

高低差がある敷地を結ぶスロープ
The slope which connects the stepped site

軒先の緑道と連続する鉢植
Flower pots continue to the green passage

住み手の暮らしがにじみ出す住棟の軒先
Use of the space under the eaves shows the lifestyle of the inhabitants

住戸の屋外デッキが連続する緑道
The exterior decking continues out to the green passage

Yokosuka Kamoi Public Housing

2009

065

A room open to the green passage

The flat floor of the common area generated by the underside beam system

1. 集会所
2. 児童公園
3. 生活相談室
4. 川
5. ペデストリアンデッキ
6. 公道
7. バス停

1. Assembly Room
2. Children's Park
3. Elderly Counseling Room
4. River
5. Pedestrian Deck
6. Public Road
7. Bus Stop

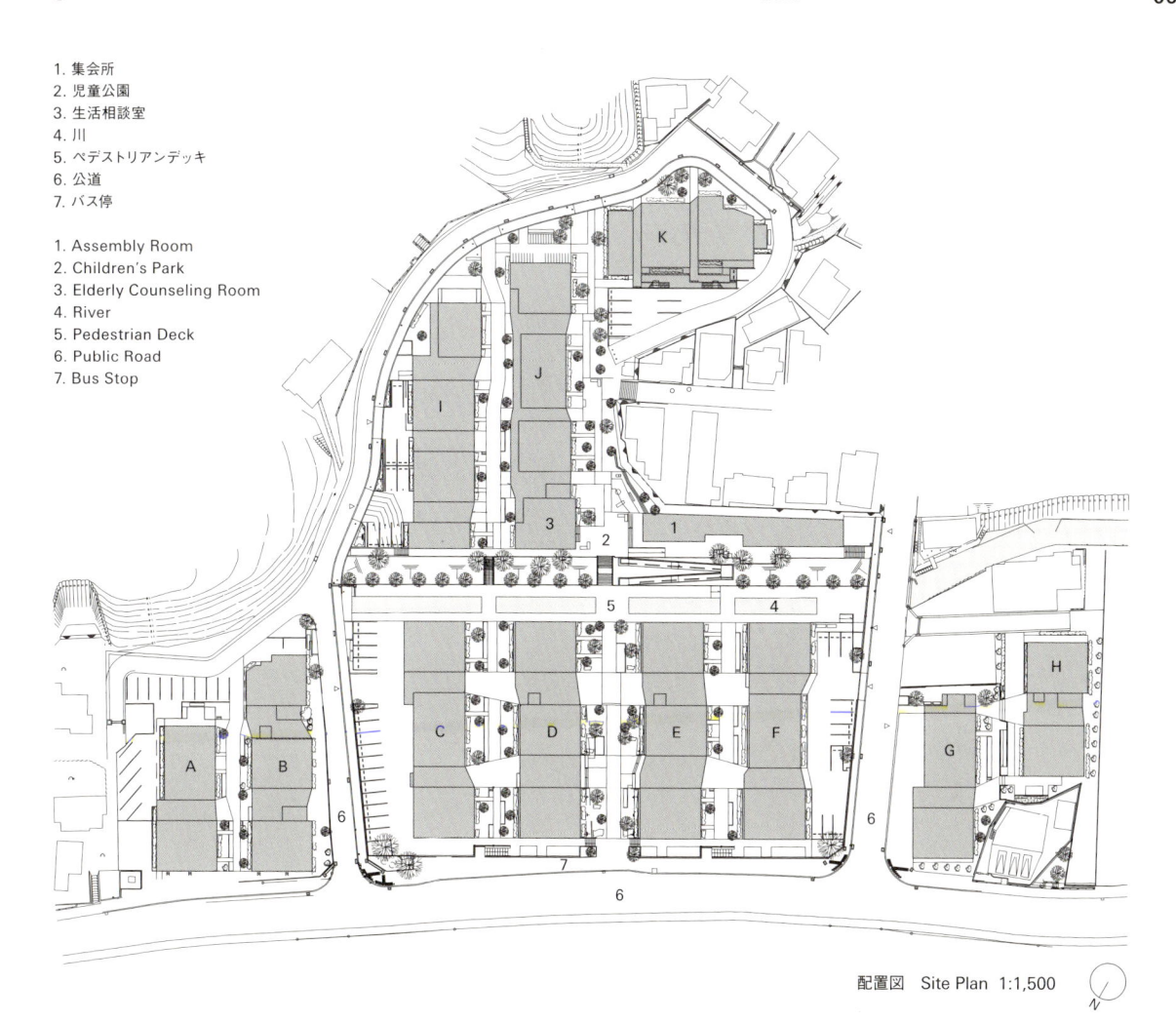

配置図　Site Plan 1:1,500

用途:市営住宅団地
設計期間:2002/11-2005/01
施工期間:
1期(A·B·G·H棟)＝2005/02-2006/03
2期(I·J·K棟)＝2006/01-2007/02
3期(C·D·E·F棟)＝2008/01-2009/02
場所:神奈川県横須賀市
延床面積:10,199.00㎡
構造:RC造＋鉄骨造
階数:
A·B·G·H棟＝3/0
I·J·K棟＝2/0
C·D·E·F棟＝3/0
＊J棟はシルバーハウジング

Use: Public Housing
Design Period: 11/2002-01/2005
Construction Period:
First Term (Annex A, B, G, H)=02/2005-03/2006
Second Term (Annex I, J, K)=01/2006-02/2007
Third Term (Annex C, D, E, F)=01/2008-02/2009
Location: Yokosuka City, Kanagawa
Total Floor Area: 10,199.00㎡
Structure: Reinforced Concrete+Steel Frame
Floors:
Annex A, B, G, H=3/0
Annex I, J, K=2/0
Annex C, D, E, F=3/0
＊Annex J is senior citizen housing

半居
HANKYO

2009

屋上から夜明けの琵琶湖を望む
View of Lake Biwa from the roof top at dawn

半居

京都の建築プロジェクトで関西に出向いた飯田が、滋賀県湖西地区の風景に魅せられて土地を購入。自らのセカンドハウスを建設した。それがこの「半居」である。

敷地は琵琶湖のほとりだが、湖周道路を挟んで少し陸側に入り込んでいる。湖への眺望を得るために、建物を可能なかぎり高くし、屋上を設けた。小住宅ながら、外観が塔のように縦長となっているのはそのためである。

建物ボリュームのほとんどを占めるのは、2階のレベルに設けられたリビング・ダイニング・キッチンだ。その上部にロフトがあり、FRPグレーチングの床とOSB合板の床がズレながら重なっている。これにより、全体をワンルームとして感じさせながらも、多様な場所を内部に実現している。最小限のスペースだが、窮屈ではない。

材料や工法の選択においてはローコストを追求。雨風をしのぐだけの最低限の機能を備えるにとどめている。構造は木造で、同じ規格材を柱と梁の両方に使用。これに金属のロッドを組み合わせて剛性を確保した。

建物名には、「住居には満たない何か」だからという意味が込められている。しかし、飯田作品の多くで、2棟が対になって建てられてきたことを思い起こせば、本来ならもう1棟があるはずなのに、ここではそれがないから「半居」なのである、と解釈することも可能だろう。

HANKYO

When he visited the Kansai area for a project in Kyoto, Mr. Iida was attracted by the scenery at the west of Lake Biwa in Shiga prefecture and bought a piece of land there. He designed his own second house, 'HANKYO.'
Even though this site is at the side of Lake Biwa, it is across the road and slightly removed from the water. In order to gain a view of the lake, the building is elevated as much as possible and has a rooftop terrace. Therefore, despite being a small house, the exterior appearance is tall like a tower.
Most of the volume is occupied with a living, dining and kitchen area on the second floor. The loft space is above them and the FRP grating floor and OSB plywood floor are offset and overlapping. And this arrangement realized a variety of spaces inside, even though it is a one room space overall. It is minimal but not tight.
The selection of materials and construction methods was driven by cost. Only the minimum level of functions to avoid rain and wind was set up. The structure is timber and the same standard size timber is used for both columns and beams. In order to establish structural rigidity, steel rods were also used.
The name of this project has a meaning of 'something less than residence.' However thinking of Mr. Iida's other projects, some of them have twin annexes. Therefore it is possible to interpret that there should be one more annex but it's not here, so this is a 'HANKYO' (half residence).

南東側の全景
View from the south east

北側の外観
View from the north

壁が全開する1階の土間
The doma (an exterior surface continuing inside) on the first floor where all the walls are open

2階の生活空間
The living space on the second floor

2階の吹き抜け
The double height space on the second floor

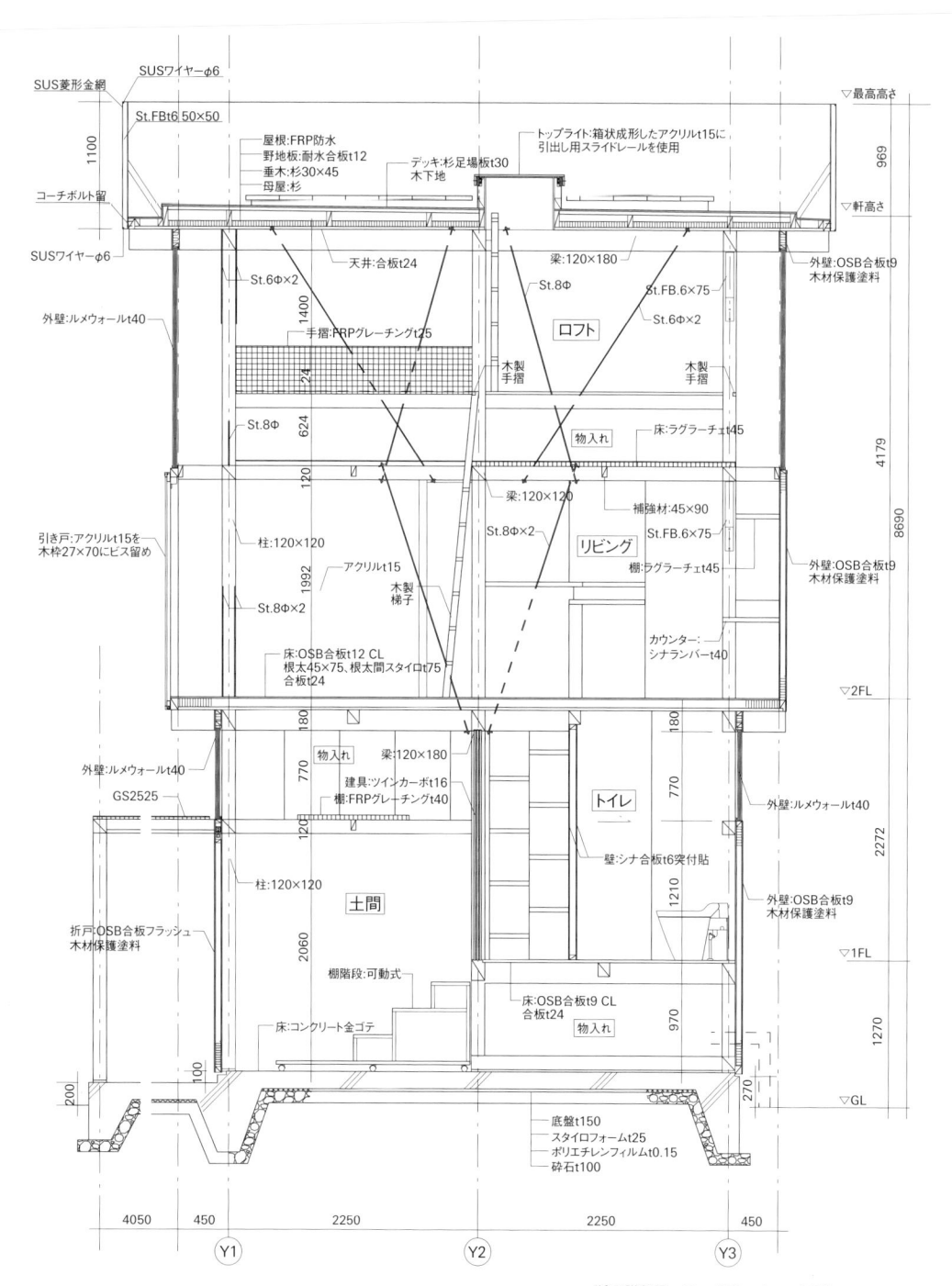

断面詳細図　Detail Section　1:50

ロフト階から2階を見下ろす
Looking down to the second floor from the loft

室内が透ける夕景
Night view seeing into the interior

HANKYO

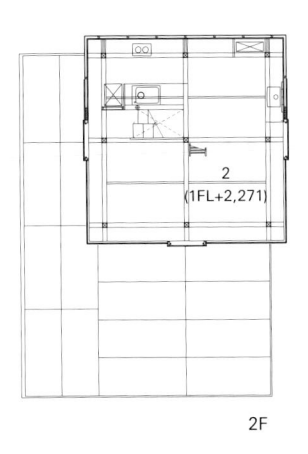

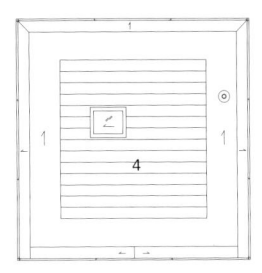

2
(1FL+2,271)

2F

(1FL±0)

1F

1
(GL+300)

1
(GL+200)

土間レベル
Doma Level

屋上階
Loft Floor

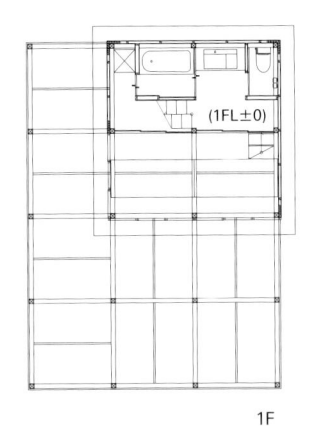

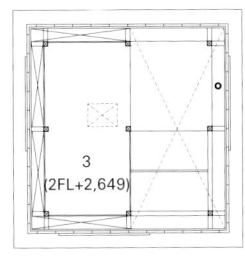

3
(2FL+2,649)

ロフト階
Loft Floor

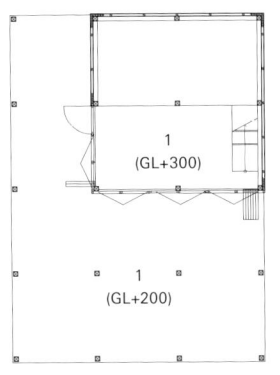

1. 土間
2. リビング
3. ロフト
4. テラス

1. Doma (Concrete Slab)
2. Living Room
3. Loft
4. Roof Deck

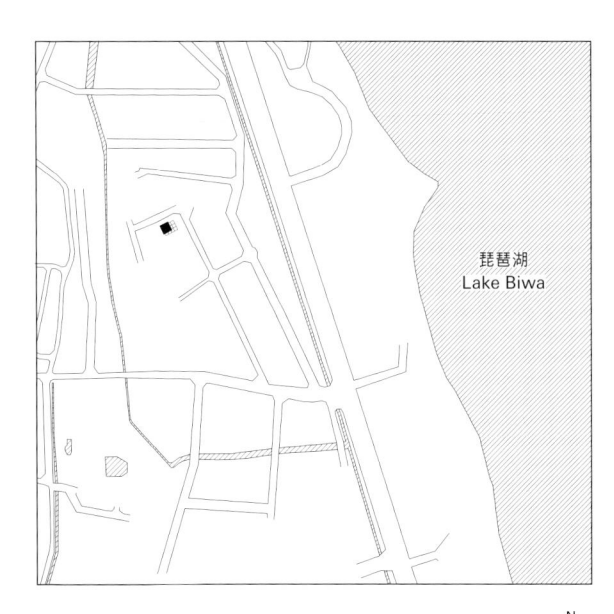

平面図　Plan 1:200

琵琶湖
Lake Biwa

配置図　Site Plan 1:5,000

用途:別荘	Use: Second House
設計期間:2008/08-2009/03	Design Period: 08/2008-03/2009
施工期間:2009/06-09	Construction Period: 06-09/2009
場所:滋賀県高島市	Location: Takashima City, Shiga
延床面積:49.41㎡	Total Floor Area: 49.41㎡
構造:木造	Structure: Wood
階数:2/0	Floors: 2/0

パークハウス吉祥寺 OIKOS

Park House Kichijoji OIKOS

2010

リビングスペース
The living space

パークハウス吉祥寺OIKOS

三菱地所の分譲集合住宅。家型のボリュームの中に、9戸の住宅を納めている。

平面の計画では、厨房、トイレ、浴室などのサービススペースを住戸の中央部にコンパクトにまとめ、それ以外の主空間をできるだけ広く確保した。また、各住戸とも水回りとバルコニーを隣接させた点も特徴で、矩形の平面から突き出たところがバルコニーと洗濯機置き場になっている。バルコニーは、設備スペースや避難ルートとなるほか、物干し場としても使われる。定型化した集合住宅のプランを解体し、再構成する試みだ。

環境配慮の仕組みも太陽光発電、外断熱工法、ペアガラスの木製サッシなど、色々と取り入れている。特に注目すべきは床下チャンバー型空調方式の採用で、これは水回り部の天井裏に設置した空調ユニットでつくった暖気、冷気を、住戸内のチャンバーを通して床下から吹き出すというもの。輻射と対流を組み合わせた、建物全体を快適化する空調システムである。

Park House Kichijoji OIKOS

This is a residential project to sell by Mitsubishi Estate. There are nine residential units in this single house -form volume. Regarding the plan, the service spaces such as kitchen, toilet, bathroom etc are gathered in the center compactly to ensure the other main spaces are as free as possible. The wet area and the balcony are adjacent to each other, which is a feature, so the projected part on the rectangular plan is a balcony where a washing machine is installed. This balcony is also a space for machinery, an escape route and for hanging washing. This is a challenge, to take the standardized plan of a housing complex apart and re-construct it better. Environmental friendly devices are applied such as a solar power system, external insulation, wooden window frames with double glazing and so on. The most remarkable point is a chamber air-conditioning system under the floor which blows warm and cold air. It is an air-conditioning unit installed in the ceiling above the wet area. Air travels through the chamber within the unit and blows from the floor. This system makes the whole building comfortable with a combination of radiant and convection heating.

西側のファサード
The west facade

ロフトのある最上階
The top floor includes a loft

パークハウス吉祥寺OIKOS　　Park House Kichijoji OIKOS　　2010　　079

用途：分譲集合住宅
設計期間：2008/09-2009/10
施工期間：2009/11-2010/10
場所：東京都武蔵野市
延床面積：703.24㎡
構造：RC造
階数：4/0
共同設計：三菱地所ホーム

Use: Condominium
Design Period: 09/2008-10/2009
Construction Period: 11/2009-10/2010
Location: Musashino City, Tokyo
Total Floor Area: 703.24㎡
Structure: Reinforced Concrete
Floors: 4/0
Collaborator: Mitsubishi Estate Home

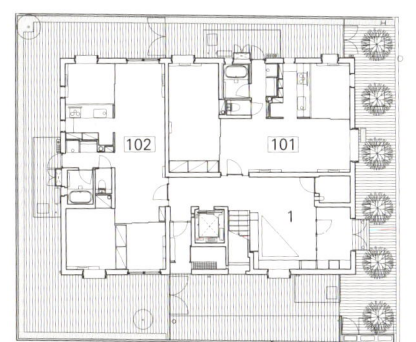

1階のエントランスロビー
The entrance lobby on the first floor

1. エントランスロビー
1. Entrance Lobby

1F 平面図　1F Plan　1:300

2F 平面図　2F Plan

3F 平面図　3F Plan

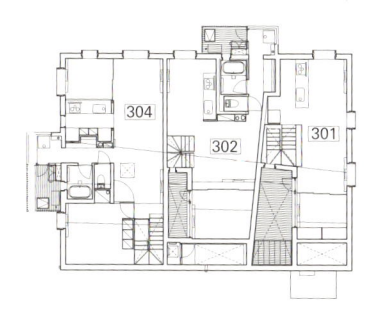

4F 平面図　4F Plan

新潟高田の家

House in Takada

2011

新潟高田の家

新潟県の豪雪地に建つ住宅である。この地域では多い年には2mの積雪となる。屋根に積もった雪を下ろすために、通常の家屋では年に3〜4回の雪下ろしをすることが必要という。これは高齢者が住むには、大変大きな負担となる。こうした雪国の住宅が抱える問題を解決することが、この住宅のテーマとなった。

特徴は鉄筋コンクリート造の屋根。降雪をセンサーが感知すると、そこに設けられたパイプから井戸水を散水して雪を溶かす。溶かした雪を流すべく、屋根は1枚の板を折り曲げて、連続したゆるい斜面をつくり上げている。それはまるで地形のようである。

内部には、屋根のかたちが天井高さの変化となってそのまま現れ、高齢の建築主に配慮してバリアーを最小限化したワンルーム的空間を、さりげなく分節している。深夜電力を利用した床暖房など、省エネルギーと快適さを両立させる設備の工夫も凝らした。

House in Takada

This is a house located in a heavy snowfall area in Niigata. This area has 2m falls of snow, when it snows heavily. Usually snow shoveling from the roof is required three or four times a season on a typical house. This is a big task for elderly people. Solving this problem which many houses in snow areas face became a theme when designing this house.

The feature of this house is the RC roof. When the sensor detects the snow, well water is sprinkled from piping on the roof and this water melts the snow. One sheet of roof is bent and creates a continuous gentle slope to run the snow off the roof. It is a kind of geography.

The shape of the roof appears as a difference of the ceiling height inside of the house, and it divides the one room space underneath informally where the barrier is minimized for elderly clients. He also employed measures to achieve both energysaving and comfort by using a floor heating system which only uses cheaper night-time energy.

折れ曲がったコンクリート屋根の形がわかる全景（竣工時）
The entire building showing the folded concrete roof upon completion

南側、庭から見た外観
View from the garden to the south

玄関から見た室内
Interior view from the entrance

新潟高田の家　House in Takada　2011　083

北側外観
View from the north

融雪に使う鉄分を含んだ井戸水で赤錆色に染めた屋根（竣工1年後）
The concrete roof one year later dyed red by the high iron content of the local well water used to melt winter snow

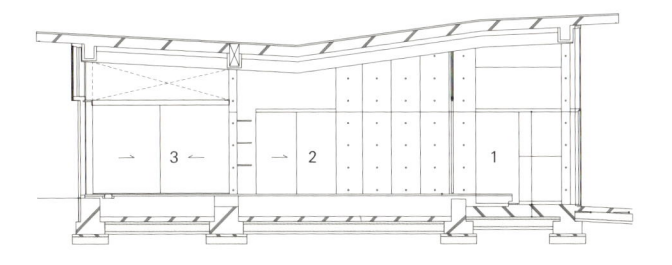

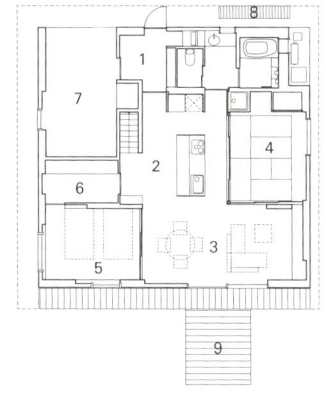

1. 玄関
2. キッチン
3. リビング
4. 和室
5. 寝室
6. 納戸
7. 駐車場
8. 融雪口
9. テラス

1. Entrance
2. Kitchen
3. Living Room
4. Japanese Room
5. Bedroom
6. Storage
7. Parking
8. Snow-melt Water Tank
9. Terrace

用途：住宅
設計期間：2011/01-05
施工期間：2011/06-10
場所：新潟県上越市
延床面積：90.55㎡
構造：RC造＋木造
階数：1/0

Use: Residence
Design Period: 01-05/2011
Construction Period: 06-10/2011
Location: Joetsu City, Niigata
Total Floor Area: 90.55㎡
Structure: Reinforced Concrete+Wood
Floors: 1/0

断面図　Section 1:150　　平面図　Plan 1:300

沖縄県看護研修センター

Okinawa Nursing Training Center

2013

沖縄県看護研修センター

保険、医療、福祉の施設が集まる那覇市近郊のメディカルゾーンに完成した、看護職者のための研修施設である。公開プロポーザルにより、飯田善彦の設計案が選ばれた。

敷地は南北で8mの高低差がある。これを生かして断面を計画し、1階の交流ゾーン、2階の事務・管理ゾーン、3～4階の研修ゾーンが段状にずれながら重なっている。各階とも南側が半外部のラウンジになっていて、異なる機能を緩やかに結びつける効果を生み出した。また駐車スペースが様々なレベルにあり、アクセスのしやすさとバリアフリーを達成している。

前面広場から見上げた際、外観を印象づけるのは3枚が重なった大屋根。これが沖縄の強い日差しから内部の環境を守る。屋根の裏側は風の道となって、自然換気を行う。また北側からの安定した自然光を採り込むことにより、昼間は照明なしでも明るい。

東西のファサードはダブルスキンとし、外側は花ブロックを積んだ壁で直射日光を遮る。また、クールチューブ、屋根面のパネルによる太陽光発電、陸屋根部の屋上緑化など、沖縄の気候風土や、傾斜地という敷地条件を生かした、環境配慮対策が採られた。

Okinawa Nursing Training Center

This is a training center for nurses located in a medical zone where insurance, medical and welfare related facilities gather near Naha city. Mr. Iida's proposal has been selected by an open proposal competition.

The site has an 8m height difference from south to north. In section this project planned to make use of this height difference with "skip-floors" the exchange zone on the first floor, the office and management zone on the second and the training zone on the third and fourth floors are offset like stairs. The lounges at the south on each floor are half outside and they help to gently connect the different functions. Since the parking spaces are at various levels, it achieves good access and is barrier free.

The three big roofs overlapping each other bolster the image of the exterior when people look up from the square in the front, and they protect the interior environment from the strong Okinawan sun. The large roof works to shade and also the space behind the roof becomes a wind path facilitating natural ventilation. Since stable natural daylight from the north is taken in, the inside is bright enough without lighting at daytime.

By making use of the Okinawan climate and the sloping site, environment-conscious measures were taken such as cooling tubes, solar panels and roof greening on the flat roofs, a double skin on the east and west facades and the stacked breezeway blocks on the exterior to shade the direct sunlight.

南東側から見た全景
View from the south east

東側のファサード
The east facade

イベント広場と連続するカフェ・ラウンジ
The café lounge connects to the outdoor event space

4階学習ラウンジから段状の吹き抜け空間を見下ろす
Looking down the stepped multi-height space from the learning lounge on the fourth floor

1階、カフェ・ラウンジ
Café lounge on the first floor

各階のラウンジが連なる段状の吹き抜け空間。
屋根と自動開閉サッシにより制御されている
The stepped multi-height space where
the lounges on each floor overlap and
where the space is controlled by the roof
and the automatic windows

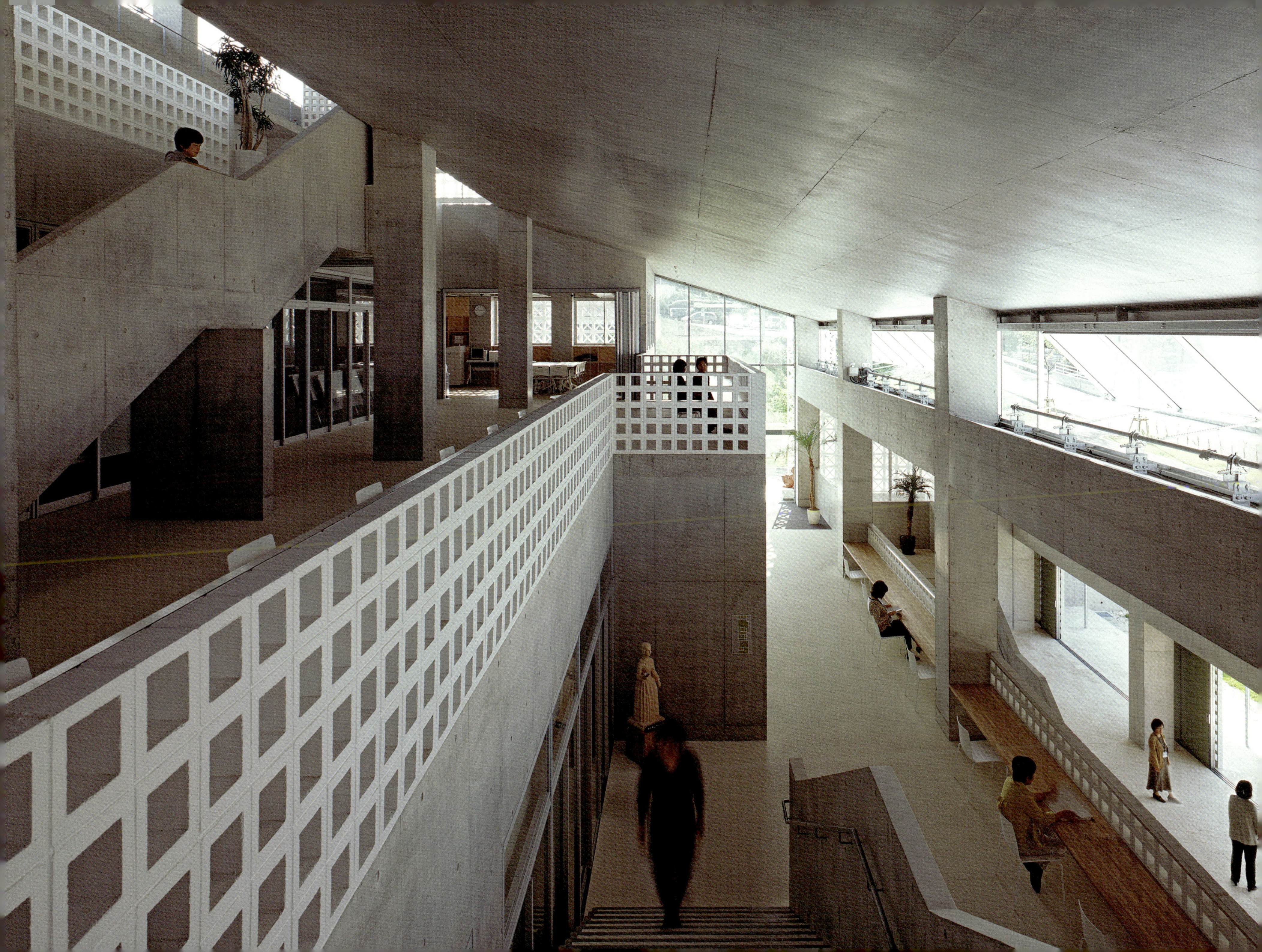

1階のラウンジから段状の吹き抜け空間を見上げる
Looking up the stepped multi-height space from the lounge on the first floor

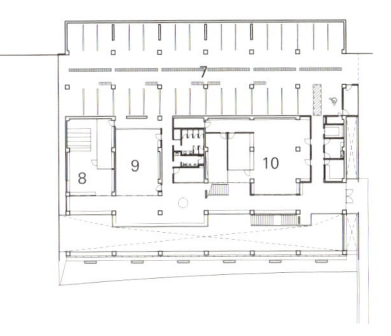

Okinawa Nursing Training Center

2F 平面図　2F Plan

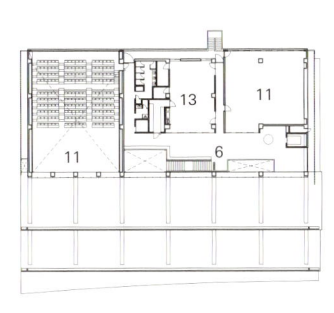

4F 平面図　4F Plan

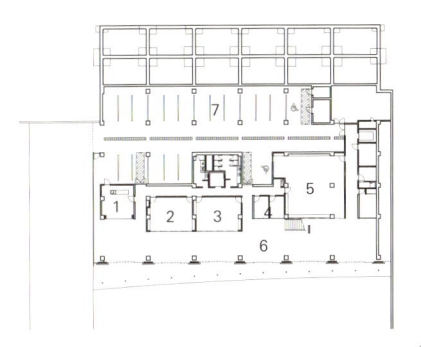

1F 平面図　1F Plan　1:1,200

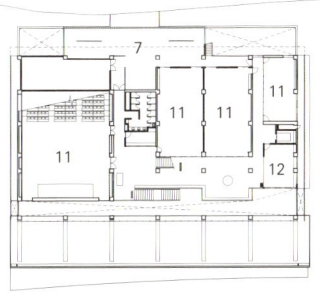

3F 平面図　3F Plan

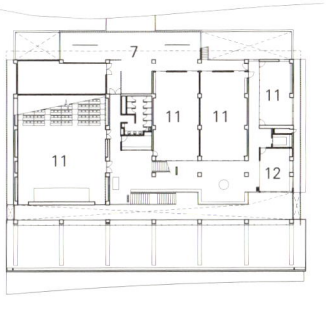

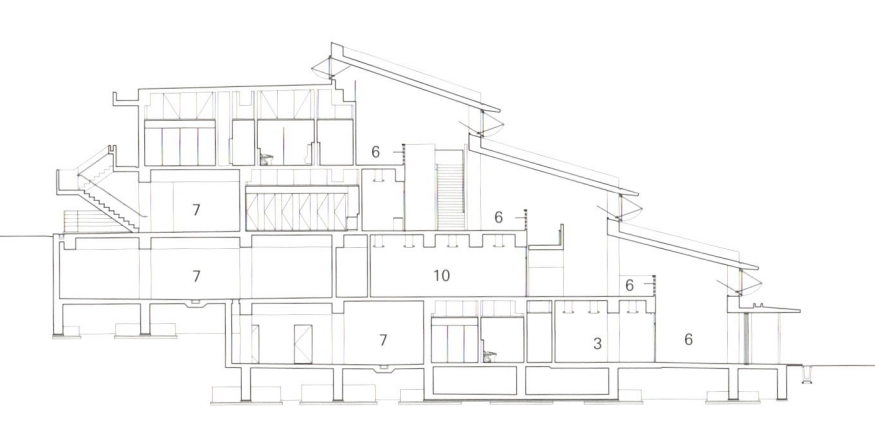

3階にある350人研修室
The training lecture room on the third floor with seating for 350

断面図　Section 1:400

1. 多目的室
2. まちの保健室・交流室
3. ナースセンター
4. 相談室
5. 訪問看護ステーション
6. ラウンジ
7. 駐車場
8. 図書室
9. 会議室
10. 事務室
11. 研修室
12. OA視聴覚室
13. 技術演習室

1. Multi-purpose Room
2. Town Nurse Station
3. Nurse Center
4. Counseling Room
5. Home Visit Nurse Station
6. Lounge
7. Parking
8. Library
9. Meeting Room
10. Office
11. Seminar Room
12. Audiovisual Room
13. Training Room

用途：研修施設＋事務所
設計期間：2011/07-2012/05
施工期間：2012/10-2013/12
場所：沖縄県島尻郡
延床面積：4,377.49㎡
構造：RC造＋SRC造
階数：4/0

Use: Training Institute+Office
Design Period: 07/2011-05/2012
Construction Period: 10/2012-12/2013
Location: Shimajiri-gun, Okinawa
Total Floor Area: 4,377.49㎡
Structure: Reinforced Concrete+Steel Framed Reinforced Concrete
Floors: 4/0

東側外観（1/30模型）
The east elevation (1/30 scale model)

京都府立新総合資料館（仮称）

京都府立総合資料館は、国宝を含む重要な古文書や府の行政文書などの資料を保存し、展示を行う施設。これを府立大学の農場跡地に移転させ、府立大学の文学部と附属図書館、新設の国際京都学センターを複合した施設として、建設するプロジェクトである。公開コンペにより、飯田善彦の設計案が選ばれた。

収容する複数の機能を、東西に長いブロックに分けて平行に配置。その間を動線が縦横に貫く。アプローチは、周囲の各方向から可能。条坊制に基づいた京都の歴史的街並みとの連続性を保ったプランである。

その全体を大屋根が覆う。京都の街の風景をつくり上げているのは寺社の大屋根だと飯田はとらえ、それを京都の新しい公共空間のかたちとして受け継ごうとしたものだ。

しかしその屋根は象徴性のみを託された一体の大屋根ではない。細やかに分節されていて、場所ごとに太陽光発電、ライトシェルフ、自然採光、自然換気など、環境配慮の技術が組み込まれている。しかも素材は、亜鉛複合板。伝統性と先端的な環境技術をハイブリッドした屋根なのだ。

内装には、京友禅、西陣織、北山丸太、京畳など、地元産の様々な材料が仕上げに参加する。それ自体が京都を表現する建物ともなっている。

Kyoto Prefectural Library and Archives [tentative name]

The Kyoto Prefectural Library and Archives is a facility to reserve and exhibit precious ancient documents including national treasures and prefectural administrative documents. This is the project to transfer the facility to the pastoral site of Kyoto Prefectural University and build a complex facility for a department of literature and library of the university and International Kyoto Learning Center. Mr. Iida Yoshihiko's design was selected by an open competition.

The multiple functions are laid in long blocks east to west, and parallel to each other. Pedestrian traffic penetrates between the blocks extensively and people can approach from various directions. The grid pattern plan maintains a continuity with the historical Kyoto street scape.

Large roofs cover the entire project. Mr. Iida proposed the large roofs of temples and shrines as the item which signifies the landscape of Kyoto and intended to present it as a form of new public space in Kyoto. However the roofs are not just a symbol but have several environment-conscious functions installed, such as solar panels, light shelves, natural daylighting and ventilation. And the material is zinc composite panel. This is a hybrid roof of tradition and advanced environmental technologies.

Traditional local materials are used for the interiors such as Kyoyuzen, Nishijinori, Kitayama cedar log, Tatami etc. The building itself expresses Kyoto.

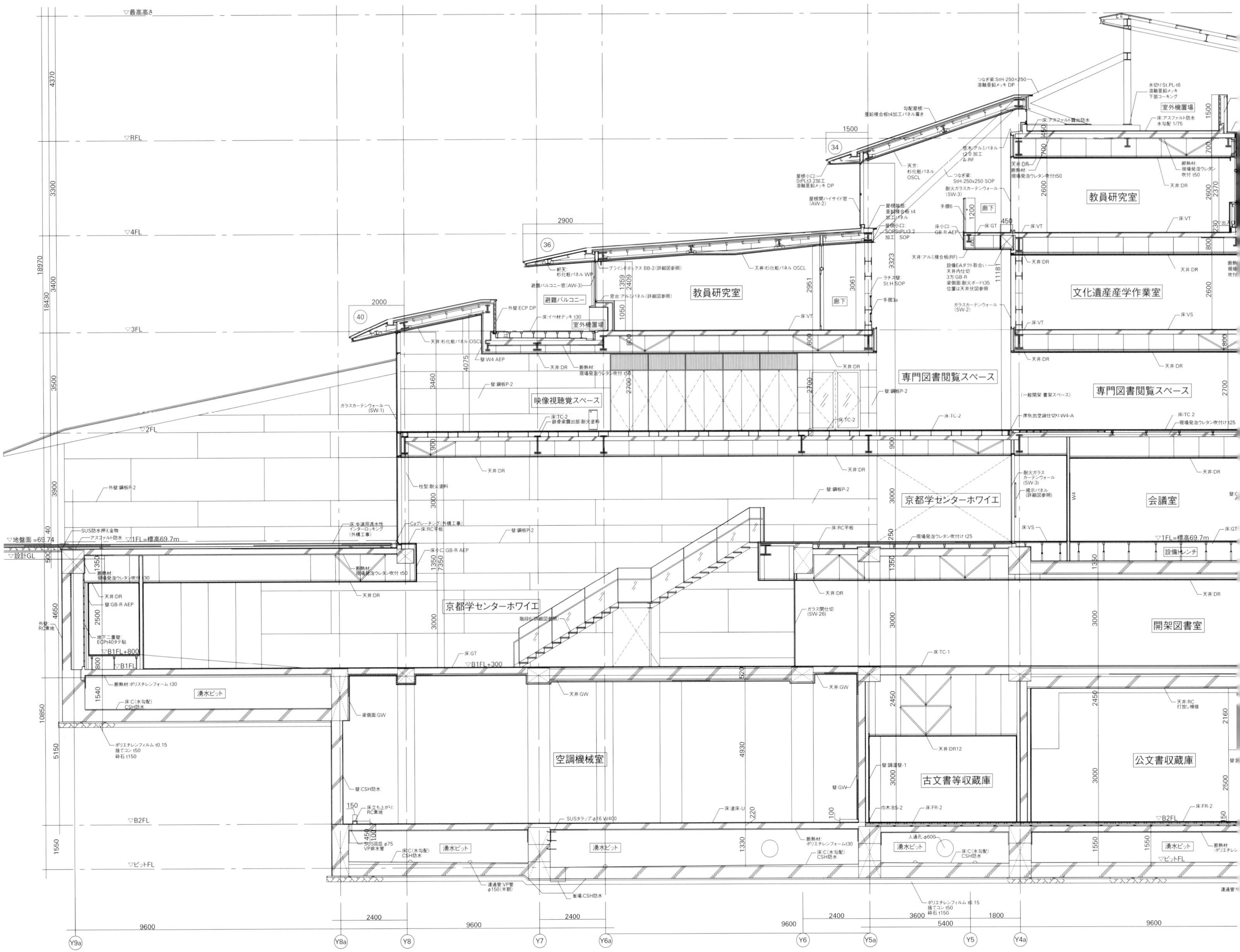

教員研究室
避難バルコニー
室外機置場
映像視聴覚スペース
廊下
専門図書閲覧スペース
文化遺産産学作業室
京都学センターホワイエ
会議室
開架図書室
湧水ピット
空調機械室
古文書等収蔵庫
公文書収蔵庫
設備トレンチ
▽最高高さ
▽RFL
▽4FL
▽3FL
▽2FL
▽1FL=標高69.7m
▽地盤面=69.74
▽設計GL
▽B1FL
▽B2FL
▽ピットFL
Y9a
Y8a
Y8
Y7
Y6a
Y6
Y5a
Y5
Y4a

095

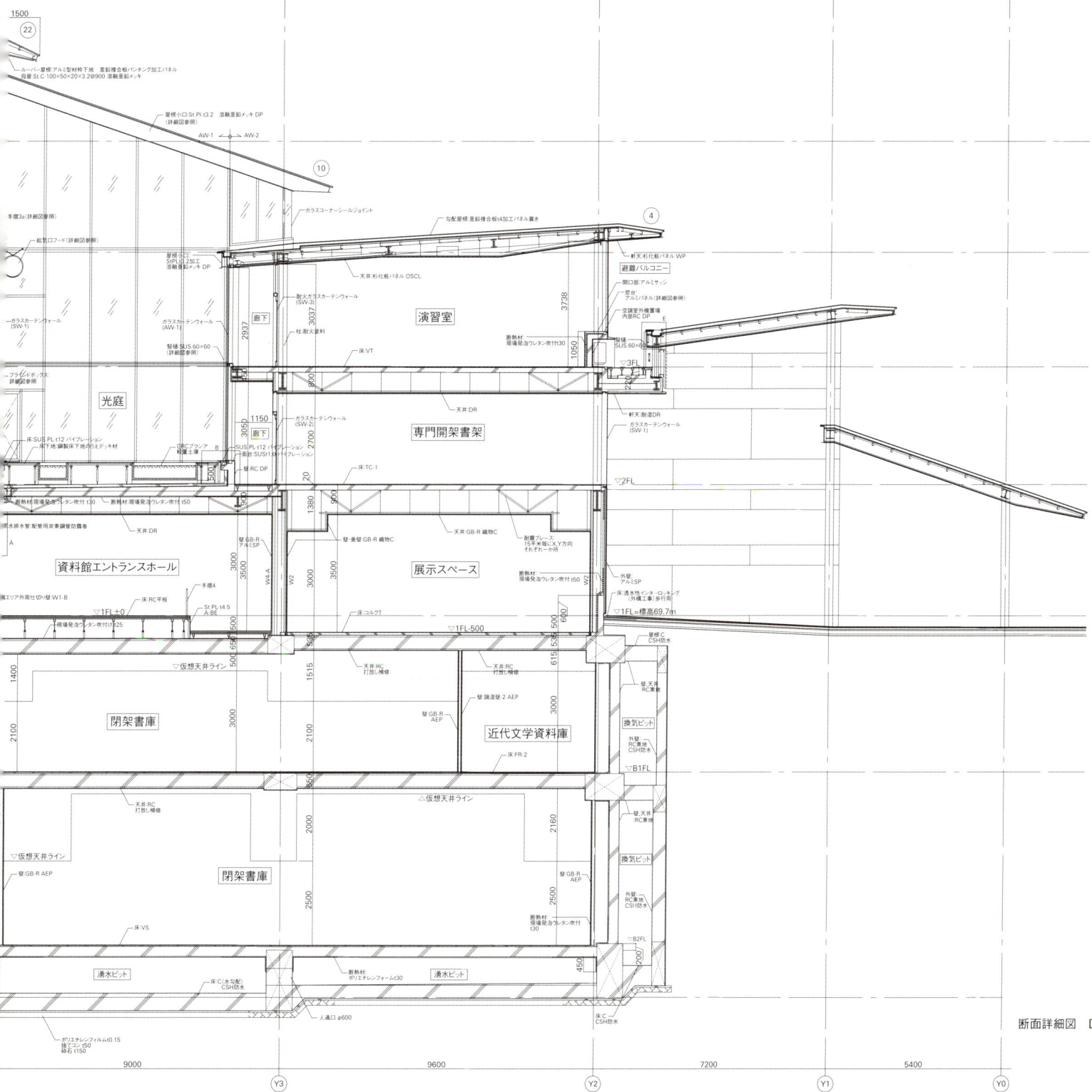

3階の通路から図書室を望む（パース）
The perspective rendering of the library viewed from the walkway on the third floor (CG)

用途：大学＋図書館＋資料館
設計期間：2011/10-2012/12
施工期間：2013/08-2015/12（予定）
場所：京都府京都市
延床面積：23,933.22㎡
構造：RC造＋SRC造＋鉄骨造
階数：4/2

Use: University+Library+Museum
Design Period: 10/2011-12/2012
Construction Period: 08/2013-12/2015
(Scheduled Completion)
Location: Kyoto City, Kyoto
Total Floor Area: 23,933.22㎡
Structure: Reinforced Concrete+Steel Framed
Reinforced Concrete+Steel Framed
Floors: 4/2

断面詳細図　Detail Section　1:160

写真クレジット

阿野太一｜名古屋大学野依記念学術交流館・野依記念物質科学研究館、
　　　　龍谷大学深草キャンパス修景計画
飯田善彦建築工房｜ピア赤レンガ(p.035のみ)、新潟高田の家(p.083右のみ)
石川奈都子｜京都府立新総合資料館(仮称)
石黒守｜川上村林業総合センター 森の交流館、北総花の丘公園 花と緑の文化館
　　　　(p.014のみ)、逗子K邸
新建築社写真部｜ピア赤レンガ(p.035を除く)
鈴木研一｜名古屋大学理学南館・理農館、パークハウス吉祥寺OIKOS、
　　　　新潟高田の家(p.083右を除く)、沖縄県看護研修センター
田中宏明｜蓼科斜楼
畑拓｜北総花の丘公園 花と緑の文化館(p.014を除く)
藤塚光政｜龍谷大学新1号館、京急高架下文化芸術施設 日ノ出スタジオ、
　　　　横須賀市営鴨居ハイム、半居

Photo Credits

Daici Ano | Nagoya University Noyori Conference Hall, Noyori
　　　　Materials Science Laboratory; Ryukoku University Fukakusa
　　　　Campus Landscape Project
IIDA ARCHISHIP STUDIO | Pier AKA-RENGA (only p.035), House in
　　　　Takada (only p.083 right)
Natsuko Ishikawa | Kyoto Prefectural Library and Archives [tentative
　　　　name]
Mamoru Ishiguro | Kawakami Forest Club, Hokuso Flower Park
　　　　Center (only p.014), Zushi K House
Shinkenchiku-sha | Pier AKA-RENGA (except p.035)
Ken'ichi Suzuki | Nagoya University Science South Building, Science
　　　　and Agricultural Building; Park House Kichijoji OIKOS, House in
　　　　Takada (except p.083 right), Okinawa Nursing Training Center
Hiroaki Tanaka | Tateshina SHARO
Taku Hata | Hokuso Flower Park Center (except p.014)
Mitsumasa Fujitsuka | Ryukoku University Building 1, Hinode Studio,
　　　　Yokosuka Kamoi Public Housing, HANKYO

そこでしかできない建築を考える｜プロジェクツ
飯田善彦

2014年10月31日　初版第1刷発行

発行者
高木伸哉

発行所
株式会社フリックスタジオ
〒106-0044 東京都港区東麻布2-28-6
電話：03-6229-1501　Fax：03-6229-1502

作品解説
磯達雄

編集
株式会社フリックスタジオ
(磯達雄＋高木伸哉＋田畑実希子)

編集協力
株式会社飯田善彦建築工房(横溝惇)
丸山純恵

デザイン
株式会社ラボラトリーズ(加藤賢策)

翻訳
ピーター・ボロンスキー

印刷・製本
藤原印刷株式会社

本書掲載内容を著作権者の承諾なしに無断で転載(翻訳、複写、インターネットでの掲載を含む)することを禁じます。

© 2014, Yoshihiko Iida + IIDA ARCHISHIP STUDIO Inc./flick studio Co., Ltd.
ISBN 978-4-904894-21-7

Thinking of an Architecture for Nowhere but Here: Projects
Yoshihiko Iida

Date of Publication
October 31, 2014

Published by
flick studio Co., Ltd./Shinya Takagi
2-28-6 Higashi-azabu, Minato-ku, Tokyo-106-0044
Phone: +81-(0)3-6229-1501　Fax: +81-(0)3-6229-1502

Annotated by
Tatsuo Iso

Edited by
flick studio Co., Ltd.
(Tatsuo Iso, Shinya Takagi, Mikiko Tabata)

Editorial Support by
IIDA ARCHISHIP STUDIO Inc. (Atsushi Yokomizo)
Sumie Maruyama

Designed by
LABORATORIES Co., Ltd. (Kensaku Kato)

Translated by
Peter Boronski

Printed by
Fujiwara Printing Co., Ltd.

All rights reserved. No part of this book may be reproduced or utilized in any form or by any information storage or retrieval system, without prior permission in writing from the copyright holders.